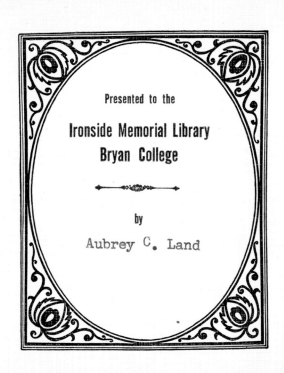

The Old Salem Series

The Moravian Potters in North Carolina by John Bivins, Jr.
The Quiet People of the Land: A Story of the North Carolina Moravians in Revolutionary Times
by Hunter James

The Quiet People of the Land *was financed in part by a grant from the American Revolution Bicentennial Administration and with the cooperation of the North Carolina Bicentennial and the Winston-Salem/Forsyth County Bicentennial Commission.*

The Quiet People
of the Land

The Quiet People
of the Land

A Story of the North Carolina Moravians
in Revolutionary Times

by Hunter James

Illustrations by Jim Stanley

*Published for
Old Salem, Inc., Winston-Salem, N.C.
by The University of North Carolina Press,
Chapel Hill, N.C.*

Library of Congress Cataloging in Publication Data
James, Hunter.
    The quiet people of the land.

    (Old Salem series)
    Bibliography: p.
    Includes index.
    1. Moravians in North Carolina. 2. North Carolina
    —Church history. I. Old Salem, Inc., Winston-Salem,
    N. C. II. Title. III. Series.
    BX8567.N8J35   284'.6756   75-44042
    ISBN 0-8078-1282-X

For MARY ELLEN

Contents

Foreword

There is nothing in the records to indicate that fundamentally the Moravians in the eighteenth and early nineteenth centuries were any more saintly or any more gifted than a great many other hardy souls in the Carolina backcountry at that time. But the Moravians who came to North Carolina from Pennsylvania and central Europe had brought with them a heritage firmly rooted in practical religion. Moreover, here, in what was then wilderness, they had installed a highly organized system of community life that was unique even in its time. The religion and the system blended in these Moravian settlements to create a climate in which ordinary men and women could, and did, rise to uncommonly high levels of accomplishment in the crafts, music, education, architecture, town government, business enterprise, and everyday Christian living.

The Moravians who settled in North Carolina traced their faith to the Bohemian martyr John Hus, who was burned at the stake in 1415 for daring to lift the Scriptures above the canons of the Church. In one of the first Protestant moves, Hus's followers formed the Unitas Fratrum (Unity of Brethren), which, despite intermittent persecution, spread across Bohemia, Moravia, and Poland. Eventually, however, the Brethren were forced into hiding. In the early 1700s, a few escaped from Moravia (hence the popular name "Moravian") and found refuge on the estate of a Saxon nobleman, Count Nicolaus Ludwig von Zinzendorf. There the Unity was reborn, and in their new town, Herrnhut, the Moravians developed many of the unique practices that were to influence so strongly their life in North Carolina.

It was a way of life grounded on a simple "heart" religion in which the making of shoes, the grinding of corn, and the playing of a musical instrument served the cause of the Lord no less directly than ministering to the heathen. The Unity served as protector and director of both the material and spiritual affairs of its members, and if a Brother could not live comfortably under that thick canopy, he was free to leave; indeed, he was invited to do so.

Herrnhut had been in operation scarcely a dozen years when the Moravians began to send colonists to America. The first settlement, in Georgia, was soon abandoned and Moravian strength concentrated in Pennsylvania, with Bethlehem as the central town. The Brethren quickly earned such a fine reputation as responsible colonists that in the early 1750s Lord Granville of England gladly sold them a tract in what is now piedmont North Carolina. They named it *Wachau* (in English, Wachovia), after the ancestral estate of Count Zinzendorf in Austria.

The first company of Moravians arrived from Pennsylvania on 17 November 1753. Plans carefully made in advance called for a central industrial town as the seat of Moravian operations in Wachovia. The immediate concern, though, was survival. The settlers took refuge in an abandoned log cabin and the next day began to clear the land. They called the temporary settlement Bethabara, meaning "house of passage." But progress came slowly in this untamed land, Bethabara remaining the stronghold of the Moravians in Wachovia for nearly twenty years. During this time a second small settlement, Bethania, was established nearby, and Bethabara itself grew into a thriving community. The arrival of Frederic William Marshall in 1764 brought plans for the central town to the forefront. Marshall, who had been appointed chief officer for material affairs in Wachovia, had been educated at the university in Leipzig. His knowledgeable and strong leadership, together with the skilled planning of Christian Reuter, Moravian surveyor, were to be the main forces in bringing the town into reality.

In 1765 a site was selected at the center of the Wachovia tract, and on 6 January 1766, the first tree was felled for the new town of Salem (from the Hebrew word for "peace"). Construction proceeded much according to Reuter's plans, with important buildings grouped around an open square and the main street passing along the side of it. By April 1772, Salem was ready for occupancy, and the Brethren moved virtually en masse from Bethabara, leaving this first settlement a small rural community.

From that time until well into the nineteenth century, Salem functioned as a congregation town, in which the church was central to all activity. The church owned all the land, leasing lots to individual members who built their own homes and shops. The congregation itself owned and operated five of the major businesses—tavern, store, tanyard, pottery, mill—paying salaries and incentive bonuses to those who worked there. To a degree, other craftsmen were on their own in the making and selling of wares. In the Moravian view, however, a man's work, like his conscience, was under the direct guidance of the Lord, and consequently under the strict supervision of the various congregation boards charged with administering the Lord's way. In fact, there was little a Brother could do—in his own home, in his work, in his dealings with others—that did not come under the scrutiny of one or the other of these fatherly boards. And, as at Hernnhut, those who could not accept such controls were encouraged to seek residence elsewhere.

As a means of promoting greater spiritual growth among all men, women, and children in Salem, the congregation was divided into units known as choirs, according to age, sex, and marital status: Married People, Single Sisters, Single Brothers, Widows, Widowers, Older Girls, Older Boys, Children. Each had its own special religious events and its own responsibilities. The Single Brothers' and the Single Sisters' choirs both had their own choir houses, where the members lived together, and each had its own *Diaconie* (business organization). Within the wider bounds of the community, though, all of these choirs lived, worked, and worshipped together much as members of one large, close, and devout family. Such a closed community served both to safeguard the faith and to protect the faithful. As it happened, the system also served to build a sound economy and standards of production quite uncommon in this part of the country.

As the area surrounding Wachovia built up, and as roads grew better and state and national governments more efficient, the tightly knit congregation system of Salem became less necessary for security and less appealing to the Moravians themselves. Gradually the more rigid rules were relaxed, and by the middle of the nineteenth century Salem had ceased to function as a congregation town altogether. Today only the church, an active Protestant denomination, remains as a Moravian entity.

In the years between 1753 and the 1830s, however, the Moravians of Wachovia, minding their own business in their own unusual way, left a number of other distinct marks on the culture of this region that also have endured. Using the abundant store of written records and tangible evidence of that period, we hope in this Old Salem Series to show, at least in some measure, how broad and how durable this Moravian contribution actually was.

Frances Griffin

Acknowledgments

*I*n the writing of this book the author has been able to turn not only to the extensive records kept by the eighteenth–century Moravians but also to a great many people whose knowledge of Moravian history far exceed his own. Without the able assistance of Miss Mary Creech, archivist for the Moravian Church, Southern Province, a beginning could hardly have been made; nor could the final result have been anything but imperfect without the close analysis and many suggestions of Mrs. R. A. McCuiston, chairman of the Archives Reading Committee. In like manner, the late Bishop Kenneth G. Hamilton, a remarkable scholar, was most helpful in his attempt to illuminate some of the more obscure tenets of Moravian belief.

But to no one is the author more indebted than to Miss Frances Griffin, director of information for Old Salem, Inc. Both an authority in Moravian history and an exacting student of the English language, Miss Griffin has lived with this book almost as closely as the author and must share heavily in whatever success it may achieve.

The author is also indebted to John Bivins, Jr., former director of restoration for Old Salem, Inc.; to Gene Capps, Old Salem's director of education and interpretation; and to Dr. Fred Hobson of the University of Alabama, a friend whose wise counsel is often sought and sometimes heeded. A scholarly paper written by Mrs. Belinda Riggsbee of the Old Salem interpretive staff proved to be a useful research tool.

Others who have been more than generous with their time and help are Old Salem's costumer, Mrs. Howard Hall, whose position qualifies her as one of the world's principal authorities on early Moravian dress codes, and Miss Laura Mosley, who offered many pertinent suggestions concerning the Moravians and their pioneering medical achievements. The Reverend John Giesler, former pastor of Friedberg Moravian Church, also provided help of a rather special kind: a personal tour of all-but-forgotten highroads and wagon paths traveled by Revolutionary soldiers.

Nor would any statement of this kind be complete without some mention of the late Dr. Adelaide Fries, whose massive translations of the Moravian Records are absolutely essential to any proper understanding of early North Carolina history. Certainly without those records this book could not exist in its present form and very possibly in no form at all.

The Quiet People
of the Land

1

At Mill Gate and Tavern Door

The tiny wilderness town of Bethabara, North Carolina, an outpost of Moravian piety and Old World culture, was already a bustling place when Traugott Bagge arrived in February of 1768 to take over operation of the community store. It must have been obvious almost from the beginning that Bagge was not at all the typical backwoods storekeeper one might have expected to find in prerevolutionary North Carolina. The people of Bethabara came to know him both as an enterprising merchant and as a skilled accountant, a "useful man" who "spends most of his time in the store, where he finds much work in the books."[1] They may not have known, at least not yet, that he was also something of a classical scholar and a man fluent in English and German as well as in his native Swedish. He could even boast a certain familiarity with such obscure eastern tongues as Hebrew and Syriac.

Now almost forty years old, Bagge had been attracted to Moravian teachings at quite an early age. But like most young men in search of a lasting faith he had first to suffer many uncertainties, much travail, and many abiding fears of inconstancy before wholly committing himself to these pious and evangelical folk.

The Moravian Church or Unity of Brethren was just then enjoying a revival of its ancient apostolic faith. Earlier in the century some few members of the church, unable to escape persecution in their own land, had found refuge on Count Nicholas Lewis von Zinzendorf's Saxon estate. First with his protection and later with his guidance, they had built a retreat called Herrnhut and had begun to send out missionaries. As a teenager in the town of Göteborg, Sweden, Bagge had often joined his older and more devout brother in reading secretly from the hymnbook of the Herrnhut congregation—secretly because "at that time in Sweden the writings of the Brethren were considered heretical."[2]

He had also spent much time translating the Moravian church newsletter, the *Gemein Nachrichten*, "for use of the awakened." But he was still uncertain, still groping. In the years to come he fell out of grace and into the clutches of a companionable store clerk "who lived an evil life and did [him] much harm." While still a young man he had left Sweden to become a partner in his family's Hamburg clothing firm, with the understanding that he was to open a branch of the business in the nearby port city of Lübeck. Then came a fateful voyage to London, where he was to purchase a stock of goods for the new store. On his return to the continent he again fell into spiritual distress. He later reported that "contrary winds made the voyage rather long, and during it I could not help thinking about my life, its inconstancy and sinfulness, and how I was about to make it impossible to return to the Saviour, and what misery this would bring me, and I became anxious and ashamed. So I surrendered myself entirely to His will, finding very significant His words that men should give up father and mother, brother and sister for His sake."[3]

After arranging for the disposal of his newly purchased goods and returning to Göteborg long enough to say goodbye to his mother, pay his debts, and spurn two marriage proposals, one from a wealthy young woman who had once spurned him, Bagge set out for The Netherlands and the flourishing Moravian colony at Zeist. Accepted as one of the "awakened," he worked for a time in the congregation store and later served as *Vorsteher*[4] for a branch of the Moravian society at Fulneck, England. We do not know when his thoughts first turned to Carolina. We do know that he was the only one of the original shareholders in the Wachovia[5] land company actually to take up his deed.

With him on his trip to America was an even more prominent Moravian leader, the Reverend Frederic William Marshall, who in 1763 had been appointed chief administrator for the Wachovia settlements. Both were men of immense learning and unquestioned leadership ability. But it was Bagge even more than Marshall who was to guide the settlers through the troubled early years of the American Revolution. Marshall would be out of the country during much of this time. He would leave in 1775 to attend an international church synod in Europe and, with the outbreak of hostilities, would find it impossible to return for almost five years. These were especially critical years for the Moravians, a time when their allegiance to the new country was much in doubt and their "pacifism" held in open scorn. And with Marshall gone they would look increasingly to Bagge as a man who could argue their cause convincingly, eloquently, and with much-needed restraint.

At the time of Bagge's arrival the colony was already in a state of violent unrest and had been so for many years. During the French and Indian War, which broke out less than six months after the settlement of Bethabara, roaming bands of Cherokees had raided, burned, pillaged, kidnapped, and murdered almost at will. It was then that the Bethabara palisades had been thrown up and a refuge provided for settlers from as far away as the Dan and the upper reaches of the Yadkin. For reasons not altogether comprehensible, the Indians had never actually attacked the Bethabara stockade or Bethabara's sister village of Bethania. Yet they had often camped nearby, so close that the Bethania settlers could sometimes see the smoke of their campfires rising darkly against a background of falling snow. Why had they never attempted to burn the fort or take the villagers captive? Was it because, as some believed, that the bells rung for morning prayers and the conchshell horns blown at hourly intervals during the night had kept them frightened away?

The 1763 Peace of Paris, which ceded to Britain much of the old French empire in America, also brought an end to the Indian troubles. But now the colonists had been caught up in another menace almost as disquieting: the War of the Regulation. "It can scarcely be called a war," one observer has said, "and yet it rises above the dignity of a riot."[6] The backcountry settlers who were to become active in this movement lived not as the Moravians, in tightly knit communal villages, but scattered about the Carolina wilderness, on farms small and not so small—many of them, these farms, located within a short distance of Wachovia itself, near enough so that half a day's journey or less would bring their owners banging at the gates of the mill, at the door of the tavern, at the apothecary shop.

For many years these people had complained of excessive legal fees, exorbitant taxes, faulty land titles, grasping lawyers, corrupt sheriffs, and autocratic judges. They had complained too of laws requiring them to pay their quitrents (an old feudal levy that supposedly quit, or relieved, the settler of all other obligations to the landowner) in hard money, an item of extreme scarcity in the colony, rather than in the produce of their farms. The same laws required them not only to pay what they often did not even have but sometimes to travel many miles over poor or all-but-nonexistent roads to deliver their fees into the hands of provincial officials.

Much of the trouble originated within the bounds of the old Granville District, a political anomaly left over from the days when the colony was governed by the eight lords proprietors. The Granville District encompassed most of the northern half of North Carolina, all of the Wachovia tract and about one-eighth of the original proprietary grant. Created to satisfy the claims of Lord Carteret, Earl Granville, the only one of the proprietors who had refused to let himself be bought out by crown interests, this giant freehold eventually proved to be an encumbrance which his lordship was just as happy to be without. The problem by and large was that he lacked the political authority to match his wealth in land and timber and flourishing towns. So venal and inefficient were his land agents, and so few the means by which they might be called to account, that he was to realize few revenues and the colonists much grief from his administration.

Central to the Regulators' many complaints, both in the Granville District and elsewhere, was a system of legislative malapportionment that denied adequate representation to the backcountry. In the years between 1740 and 1755, when the rapidly expanding frontier settlements accounted for practically all the increase in North Carolina's population, the colonial assembly created almost as many new counties in the east as in the west. The eastern merchants and plantation owners who dominated the legislature also dominated all other branches of the provincial government, including the county courts, which at that time had broad administrative as well as judicial functions. Through a kind of political incest, legislators found it possible to serve also as superior court judges, justices of the peace (a then-potent office), clerks of court, registrars, or militia officers, and at the same time to control the appointment of sheriffs and other regulatory officials. One obvious effect of this iniquitous system was that the same officeholders who persecuted the colonists in court could prevent the passage of laws that would correct the situation. Against such odds, there seemed little hope for the backwoods corn-and-hog farmer.

All of these complaints came to a head and spilled over into wholesale insurrection in the years immediately preceding the Revolution. The Regulator movement had its formal beginning in 1766, the same year that the assembly authorized a controversial poll tax for construction of royal Governor William Tryon's "palace" at New Bern and less than two years before Bagge and Marshall arrived to take up their administrative duties in Wachovia. Bagge was later to look back on these years with some sympathy for the common folk. In the process he was also to recall that "as always and everywhere there were those who stirred up the mob, and added to their anger, so all kinds of base men gathered together in these Provinces . . . and undertook to call the officers of the land to account, and to force them to redress all fancied or real injustice."[7]

High on their list of grievances were the Moravians themselves. The men who formed the bulk of this movement—the fiercely independent Scotch-Irish Presbyterians and New Light Baptists who came streaming down the Great Philadelphia Wagon Road about the time the first Moravians were arriving in Carolina—seem to have taken an early dislike for their new neighbors, in part because of theological differences, possibly too because of differences in nationality and temperament, or perhaps out of envy for their economic well-being, or maybe even for reasons they could not quite articulate. They were, after all, a strange lot, these Moravians, with their solemn rites and festal days, their alien liturgies and *Singstunden*,[8] their love-feasts and hourly intercessions, their constant jabbering in a language no one could understand, their habit of welcoming guests and newcomers with the haunting wail of trombone, trumpet, and French horn. More troubling still was their seeming indifference to onerous taxes, their complacency in the face of royal oppression.

"They are a set of *Recabites* among the people of *Israel*— Forming a distinc[t] Body, different in all things from All People,"[9] wrote the Reverend Charles Woodmason, an Anglican itinerant whose praise for the industrious Moravians almost, but not quite, matched the fury with which he raged against the theologically unorthodox Presbyterians and New Lights.

The Moravian settlers, the first ones, had come south in the fall of 1753, not like the hunters and trappers who had come before, but with the design of the new town, the new civilization, already in their heads: men possessing all of the skills needed to ensure their survival in an untried wilderness. There were farmers, carpenters, millwrights, shoemakers, a baker, tailor, sievemaker, and preacher, a business manager, even a surgeon. These men, or rather their leaders before them, had taken up some of Lord Granville's best land, a land still unbelievably lush and wild, full of peavines and succulent grapes and all kinds of game, with great stands of hardwood forests—beech, hickory, oak, and maple—and chestnut trees so huge that turkeys could perch in the upper limbs safely out of reach of buckshot. There was much open land too, wild savannas and low-lying meadows and creek bottoms thick with canebrakes and willows. Much of it, the open land, was man-made, the Indians often burning off large tracts "to drive the deer to a given spot."[10] In those days the Yadkin was still a quick silvery stream abounding with "sundry sorts of fish and fowl" and fed by many "curious, bold creeks."[11] On an earlier exploratory trip to the colony the Moravian leader, Bishop August Spangenberg, had wandered for weeks through the Piedmont and "blue mountains" before discovering this tract and declaring it to be "the best left in North Carolina."[12]

Woodmason delivered even more eloquent testimony: "The Spot is not only Rich, fertile, and luxuriant, but the most

Romantic in Nature   Sir Philip Sidneys Description of Arcadia, falls short of this *real* Arcadia Georgia, Circassia, Armenia, or whatever Region it may be compared too. To this Spot Zinzindorff transplanted his Hernhutters. . . . Here they have laid out two Towns—*Bethelem* and *Bethsada*;[13] delightfully charming! Rocks, Cascades, Hills, Vales, Groves, Plains— Woods, Waters all most strangely intermixt, so that Imagination cannot paint anything more vivid."[14]

These "Hernhutters," said Woodmason, have "All things (save women) in common; and receive to their Community Persons of all Nations, Religion and Language." They had also organized themselves into a disciplined phalanx of "choirs," a term used not in the modern sense, or at least not in that sense alone, but simply to denote certain divisions within a given congregation. The choir system arose out of the belief that a close association of persons of like age, sex, or marital status would promote spiritual growth. There was a choir for married people, another for children, a third for single brothers, and still another for single sisters, a choir for older boys and a separate choir for older girls, and in like fashion a widows' choir and a widowers' choir. There was little variety of dress among these Moravians, the men wearing identical buckskin knee breeches and dark high-buttoned jackets, woolen in winter, linen in summer; the women's plain ankle-length garb also identical, in style at least if not in color. There were blues from homemade indigo dyes, oranges and rusts from madder root, reds from cochineal. They were a stern and resolute people, yet not entirely austere. They did not disdain the use of tobacco or strong drink taken in moderate amounts. And their singing! In this if in nothing else could be found the invincible and incorruptible joy of their faith.

The communal arrangement or "common housekeeping" which saw the settlers through their first years in Carolina lasted only until the founding of Salem, their central town, and for that reason has been often cited as a failure of the Marxist ideal. It was in fact a remarkable success, the key both to their survival and ultimate prosperity, enabling them to accomplish what none of them acting alone or even in a less formal cooperative spirit could possibly have accomplished in so short a time. It helped in another way too: it gave them a heightened awareness, gained through close association and shared responsibility, of what was required of them in the new land, a knowledge of tax rates, land laws, and legal procedures, so that unscrupulous sheriffs hesitated to impose charges which they knew to be excessive. In this way the Moravians were able to escape many of the abuses of which the Regulators complained. This "pilgrim economy" was never meant to endure always or even for very long, yet while it did endure the Brethren understood quite clearly that the loyalty of each man was not to himself and his family but rather to his choir and ultimately to the whole congregation. This was why land and homes were held in common, why there were no privately owned businesses in Wachovia, why the church elders, not the parents, decided what training a child would receive, what skills would best equip him for a life of service to the community.

All of this must have seemed infinitely strange to the typical Scotch-Irish pioneer. Another factor which almost certainly contributed to his suspicions was the Moravians' favored status as "an ancient Protestant Episcopal Church," a status entitling them to all of the privileges and immunities that up till this time had been reserved for members of the Anglican faith. Though all Americans of that era enjoyed a measure of religious freedom they had not found in the Old World, not all of them had the right to form their own parishes, choose their own vestrymen and church wardens, collect their own tithes, and perform their own marriage ceremonies. The Moravians, on the other hand, were able to do all of these things. For in spite of the "differences" which had attracted the attention of the Reverend Mr. Woodmason there were certain fundamental points of agreement between the Herrnhutters and the authorities of the established church, just as there were certain fundamental points of disagreement between them and such breakaway sects as the Presbyterians, Quakers, and New Lights, and not only these but countless others, most of them deriving from a reformist tradition associated with the life and work of the Swiss theologian John Calvin. The Moravians were not unsympathetic with many of the evangelical ideas of these reformers; they too had great respect for the authority of Scripture; they too understood the depravity of man and had felt the crippling power of original sin. Yet in nothing were they more outspoken and uncompromising than in their opposition to the forbidding Calvinistic doctrine of predestination. In the end it was their adherence to the old forms of religion, their emphasis on doctrinal purity, that enabled them to win the favor of Parliament and consequently to enjoy many of the advantages denied to other religious groups.

But in order to understand more fully the differences between these two groups of settlers—the "proper" Moravians on the one hand and the mostly illiterate "Irish bog trotters"[15] on the other—we must look to causes at once less subtle and more complicated than that. The Carolina foothills and river valleys had been settled against a background of revivalistic fervor known as the Great Awakening, a movement that could hardly have failed to color almost every aspect of frontier life. The atmosphere of the time was such that even minor theological disputes could often balloon into open war. But what did our bog-trotting backwoodsman care for such controversies? Saturnine, yet given to wildly emotional transports, a forerunner of today's snake handler and Holy Roller (though many of his kind grew beyond that), this fellow had neither the learning nor the inclination to engage in abstract theological debates; he left that to his betters, and when called upon to express his feelings at all was more likely to do so with the thump of a rifle butt than with a bon mot. His only reality was the reality of the frontier: the loneliness and fear and cold and dread. And his only reassurance the gospel as it had been handed down to him by the fervent apostles of John Calvin and Ulrich Zwingli. Hemmed in by darkness and the cries of panthers, he longed to hear this old sweet story preached in almost any recognizable form, whether from tree stump or lofty pulpit; he longed to get his children baptized, to have them born again and brought up in the Way; he would have all this from his own kind if possible, but if not, from some other.

The Reverend Richard Utley's experience with these settlers was probably typical. Before driving himself to an untimely grave this Moravian minister made innumerable preaching expeditions into the backcountry. On one of his trips to the Yadkin the New Lights "openly announced their opposition to his visits in that neighborhood." But on many other occasions his coming was anxiously awaited. Once, when his listeners overflowed their accustomed gathering place, "he went with them into the woods and preached under the trees." He met with similar successes while on a 1773 preaching mission along the New River in Virginia. "In all these corners of the earth," said the Wachovia diarist of this mission, "there are people who crossed the ocean with Brethren, or once lived in their neighborhood, or who went to a country school with them, and so have known the Brethren more or less well."[16]

From all this it seems obvious that the Moravians' troubled dealings with the Regulators must be laid to something more than mere theological concerns. Probably what it all came down to was a fundamental difference in attitude and economic circumstances. Most of the men and women who had settled the Carolina frontier had come south looking for cheap land and a chance to be free of the galling restraints—the boundary disputes, high consumer costs, high taxes, and overweening crown authorities—that had plagued them in the North. The Moravians, however, had come for quite different reasons: for cheap land, yes, but also to live as a "quiet people," to conduct themselves peaceably at whatever cost, and to spread their gospel throughout the length and breadth of a region that had known the footsteps of few hunters and trappers and fewer missionaries. Meantime they had begun to build and prosper in ways that must have seemed ominous to many of their neighbors. Judged by the standards of these other settlers, this submissive and highly disciplined Moravian society might have seemed almost an extension of the royal government, a symbol if not more than a symbol of all the things the Regulators thought they had left behind them in New Jersey and Maryland and Pennsylvania.

And so now they had come banging at mill gate and tavern door. The first stirrings of the American Revolution were still more than fifteen years distant when these angry farmers began resorting to direct action as an answer for their grievances. In 1759 there had been riots in Halifax County. Six years later unauthorized settlers in Mecklenburg County severely whipped and drove off a party of royal surveyors. There had been almost constant disorders, protests, and demonstrations in many other parts of the colony as well, most notably in Orange and Granville counties; and now, with the westward advance of civilization, the mood of defiance had spread to the Rowan frontier, and not least to such lively trade centers as Salisbury and Bethabara.

Even Governor William Tryon, who in spite of a certain extravagant manner was by all odds the most competent of North Carolina's colonial executives, agreed that there was merit in many of the Regulator complaints. In a 1767 letter to the earl of Shelburne he acknowledged that the sheriffs had stolen "more than one half of the public money ordered to be raised and collected by them."[17] And as long as the Regulators were content to bring their petitions before him in an orderly manner he made some effort to improve the conditions under which they lived. But by the fall of 1770, just when there was a very real prospect for legislative relief, they had become more and more impatient, more disposed to violence, and less interested in political solutions—had become convinced, in short, that Tryon's efforts were mostly a ruse and would result in little, if any, actual reform.

And so these men rose up, embattled, furious, inflamed by the bitterly satiric verse of the Regulator poet Rednap Howell and the political "advertisements" of the rustic essayist and propagandist Hermon Husbands. We have come to think of the Regulators as a gallant and resourceful band of folk heroes, as in some respects they were. But to the Moravians they and their undisciplined ways were about as "heroic" as the fevers that rode in all too frequently on the night fogs out of swamp and creek bottom. Like most movements that spring up in answer to a very real need, this one had quickly outgrown its original purpose and had begun to fatten on its own excesses. This was quite clearly the view that most Moravians formed at the time and that has come to be shared by such modern authorities as the historian Carl Bridenbaugh: "Their expressed grievances were good reason for direct action; that left unexpressed was what I conceive to have been the real or basic reason: a general reluctance to accept any bridling of their hitherto unrestricted freedom in the interest of what seems reasonable to any proponent of a well ordered society. To exchange the state of nature for the civil compact pleased them not, especially when the officials were not of their own nation and faith, and an actual payment of taxes was involved."[18]

In the winter and early spring of 1771 the Regulators were in a heady mood. There had been many rousing successes in recent months, the most dramatic of which had occurred the previous fall, when some 150 of their number had taken over the Orange County Court, dragging the hated judge and assemblyman Edmund Fanning off the bench and down the courthouse stairs, "his head striking violently on every step,"[19] and on through the streets of Hillsborough, spitting and kicking at him and beating him so brutally that one of his eyes hung loose.

The admittedly partisan accounts left by the victims or near-victims of these Regulator terrorists go on to paint an even more lurid picture: Fanning standing amid a litter of broken furniture and smashed china, his jacket splattered with blood and his periwig on wrong, and then being driven not only out of his house but out of the town, the hounds at his heels and the mob stoning him as he fled. Later there were reports that two of the Regulator chieftains, James Hunter and William Butler, had paraded naked through the streets with Fanning's "wearing clothes" held high on a wooden pole. By this time, or so it was alleged, most of the remaining courthouse officials had also been kicked, reviled, pounded, spat on, and chased out of town. And in the courthouse itself many other wild scenes were in progress. At the lawyer's bar sat a Negro prisoner, dead these several hours, executed in the name of the crown, and only this moment brought upstairs to take part in the celebration. The next day some of the rioters conducted a mock trial ridiculing the legal processes which they felt had driven them to this extremity, while on the steps outside and in the streets and indeed through the whole town there rose a mingled storm of shouts, curses, and drunken laughter.

This, however, was not the end of the matter. It became readily apparent that the Hillsborough disorders were to have other and, for the Regulators, even more disastrous consequences. Reports of the incident permanently alienated many of their more responsible followers and thus marked both the moment of their greatest triumph and the beginning of their decline. But they didn't know that yet. As the riotous

Carolina spring came on, they gathered in small groups and large bands, and then in even larger bands, and now began to contemplate a military expedition which they believed would finally bring down Governor Tryon and the whole vast array of lordly east-coast plutocrats said to have conspired with him in oppressing the common people.

The rebels also began to appear more frequently in the Moravian towns. Some months before, after learning that Bagge had supplied the governor's troops with two wagon-loads of bread, they had threatened the merchant with a whipping. This seemed only logical. They had whipped sheriffs, clerks, lawyers, judges, surveyors, and other government officials. Why not a small-town storekeeper?

Bagge managed to escape this punishment and seems to have coped reasonably well with their many other threats. In dealing with the Regulators, as with the Revolutionary leaders of later years, he was consistently generous, patient, wise, a master of all the arts of conciliation. The streak of Teutonic willfulness and dogmatism that was often to mar his relations with more intimate associates appears never to have interfered with his function as diplomat or with his occasional role of *Fremden Diener*.[20]

Because Bagge and the other Moravian leaders chose to treat the Regulator complaints with more respect than they actually deserved, Bethabara may well have been spared the kind of violence that all but wrecked Hillsborough. An entry in the Bethabara diary for 16 March 1771 describes one of these confrontations in some detail. On that date the Regulator Joseph Harris appeared in town—he and a dozen others—and peremptorily summoned Bagge, Marshall, and the physician Jacob Bonn to answer for certain misdeeds allegedly committed by the original Moravian settlers. The incident was not without its omens: "Last night a large wolf was caught in the trap near the brewery; the night before wolves came into the lane behind the shed, and would probably have broken into the sheep-fold had not the baying of the dogs brought people to drive them away. This seemed almost a prophecy of the events of the day, for this afternoon the party of Regulators from the Yadkin appeared as they had said."[21]

Their main allegation was that Jacob Loesch, Bethabara's first business manager, had measured off for himself land to which two non-Moravians had already taken title. Their spokesman, Edward Hughes, a ferry operator and former justice of the peace whom the Moravians had once rescued from the Indians, had a complaint of his own: he contended that he had paid Lord Granville's land agent, Francis Corbin, an unspecified sum of money for the land on which Bethabara was built and would need thirty pounds sterling before granting title to the Moravians. But since he had waited eighteen years to make his claim and still had no proof to back it up, the Brethren "politely and seriously" urged him to take the matter to court. They also offered to recall Brother Loesch from Pennsylvania so that the petitioners might take up their other grievances with him directly. The men never bothered to accept this offer, and Hughes apparently never bothered to take his own complaint to court. The Bethabara diarist later summed up the whole thing as a lot of "groundless babbling" and added: "They may have wanted to try whether the terrifying name of Regulator would not frighten us into giving them what they wanted."[22]

Very soon now the name would no longer be so "terrifying," and neither the Moravian colonists nor anyone else would have to bar their doors against the likes of Joseph Harris, and his querulous companions. In mid-May these men and hundreds of others who shared their feelings of outrage would move against the governor's troops in the celebrated and, for them, calamitous Battle of Alamance.

They seem never to have doubted that their cause was just and their triumph certain. Drawn up on the west bank of Alamance Creek, they outnumbered the provincial militia by almost two to one, but they were inadequately armed and without any real discipline or leadership. The one man who might have led them effectively was the Guilford County insurrectionist James Hunter, sometimes described as the "general of the Regulation." But Hunter wasn't interested. "We are all freemen," he said, "and everyone must command himself."[23] Certainly they got no help from their propagandist and chief agitator Hermon Husbands who appeared at the scene and then hastily departed before the shooting began. In subsequent days he moved furtive and hunted through the Wachovia woods and on one occasion appeared in the streets of

Bethabara. Or at least the Brethren believed it was Husbands who came to Dr. Bonn's door on the afternoon of 19 May and later shot a pursuer who had boasted "that if he could get help he would capture Husband and take him to the Governor."

On the road north of Bethania "this man met five Regulators, and one of them shot at him (very likely it was Husband who did it), but the ball passed through his waistcoat, which was open, barely scratching him. The man came at full gallop to Bethania weeping like a child, and pale as a corpse."[25]

The news of the Battle of Alamance drifted back in fragmentary and often contradictory accounts. The first full though less than accurate report was brought by the one-handed peddler Joseph Hughs. In the days to come the pieces began to fit together: how the governor had given the Regulators an hour to surrender and how at the end of that time his troops opened fire, killing nine of the "obstinate and infatuated rebels"[26] and wounding hundreds of others, how the men from Abbotts Creek, later a loyalist stronghold, had thrown down their guns, hats, and coats and fled with the first volley (or was Hughs correct when he said that they had stacked their arms and been pardoned by the governor?), how one victim had been found with part of his skull shot away and another with the lower part of his body missing, how one of the prisoners had been hanged on the battlefield while Tryon "turned aside weeping," and how the governor even now had begun his long march into the backcountry, laying waste the plantations of such Regulator leaders as Hunter and Husbands and extracting from all the combatants who had not fled far enough or fast enough an oath of allegiance to the crown—a march that before many days would bring him to Salisbury and ultimately to Bethabara.

Governor William Tryon was the unwitting embodiment of just about everything the backwoodsmen despised in their British overlords. Some thought him an imperious fop, ambitious, cold, pompous, excessively proud, too much given to gracious living, and a bit too fond of good books, fine art, music. But even if all of these things were admitted (and the portrait is almost certainly overdrawn in some degree) it must also be said that he was an accomplished military tactician and, for the time, a thoroughly enlightened statesman.

The Regulators came knocking at mill gate and tavern door

[18] THE QUIET PEOPLE OF THE LAND

His refusal to negotiate with Regulator leaders and his close friendship with the Hillsborough dandy Edmund Fanning counted heavily against him, as did his part in the building of the Tryon Palace at New Bern. The palace, erected with tax funds which added significantly to the colony's financial burden, was one of the many grievances that had brought the Regulators into the field. Tryon had lobbied extensively for these funds and had built with them an elegant state building soon to be regarded as one of the few real glories of North Carolina architecture; at the same time he had provided the colony with the answer to a long-standing need: a fixed seat of government. But his enemies saw in all this, and not without good reasons of their own, merely another example of royal extravagance.

By the time the building was ready for occupancy, in the summer of 1770, events were already building to flashpoint. After the Hillsborough riot the governor had sought legislative permission to move against the Regulators militarily and had even postponed his departure from the colony—he was shortly to become governor of New York—in order to put down their now-dangerous rebellion.

And there was no doubt that he had succeeded in that aim; the Battle of Alamance had suddenly and dramatically ended all further thought of revolt. As for the Moravians, the governor would not fail to notice that they had taken no part in the Regulator agitation, nor would he have been surprised at their refusal to do so. He had very early formed a good opinion of their loyalty. In March of 1766, less than a year after his appointment as governor, he had invited the Brethren to send one of their leaders as an emissary to his Brunswick home. They learned of the invitation through their "good old friend Mr. James Hasel," acting chief judge of the Salisbury court. The Brethren explained that spring planting was already upon them and pleaded for more time. But Judge Hasell "would take no excuse, and advised that we do not postpone the visit, giving several reasons, and among them that 'Not all people were our friends.'"[27]

This seemed to leave no room for argument. And so it was that the Reverend John Ettwein, who was leaving Bethabara in April to attend a Moravian synod in Pennsylvania, agreed to include in his travel plans a courtesy call on the governor and his wife. Tryon was exceedingly cordial and at the same time a little suspicious. He had apparently assumed that the first loyalty of the Moravian colonists was not to the province in which they lived but to their overlords in Saxony. Was it true that they habitually sent large sums of money to Europe? He raised a good many other questions about their financial obligations and commercial practices, informing his guest most emphatically "that so long as he was Governor he would not willingly see [them] send money out of the country!"[28] Assured that they had sent no money abroad except for the payment of debts and quitrents, he quickly became persuaded of their fidelity and from that time on seems to have regarded them as useful allies in his struggles with North Carolina's contentious frontiersmen.

Late the next summer Tryon had visited Bethabara purposely to find out more about these pious Brethren, and in so doing permitted his hosts to glimpse a side of his character that was to remain well hidden from the Regulators. He nodded pleasantly at everybody and seemed favorably impressed with all aspects of Moravian society. He and his wife spent considerable time strolling about the grounds, examining the workshops and farm buildings, absorbing Moravian history, and savoring the music that seemed so much a part of the life of the community. One afternoon they rode into the new town of Salem and spoke approvingly "of the regular manner in which the building had been begun." It was much the same in Bethania, where they again spoke approvingly of just about everything, "especially the many children that they saw in front of the houses." At first suspicious of Moravian "communism," the governor seemed "well satisfied" when told that a Brother could retain his personal property even though in everything else his primary obligation was to the church *Oeconomie*. Only in one thing did he remain unsatisfied: his repeated attempts to get the Moravian trade for the port towns of Brunswick and Wilmington. Ettwein had explained during his earlier audience with the governor why the Brethren were reluctant to trade in those towns: "I told him the reason was that we needed many things which could not be had in Willmington, that goods were at least ten percent higher there than in Charlestown, and that the deerskins with which we paid in Charlestown were worth more than in Willmington."[29]

Some time before leaving Bethabara the governor placed an order for 478 pounds of candles, 150 pounds of butter, 6 beehives, 3 bushels of rye, a gun, and a windmill, all of which reached him in good time but without the intended result—which was, of course, the creation of a lively and enduring trade between Wachovia and the North Carolina port areas.

In every other way his visit had been a refreshing experience. He would remember Bethabara fondly—the music, "the beautiful singing of the Sisters," the busy workshops and prosperous farms, the solemnity of the Moravian worship services—and on his next visit, in 1771, after the Battle of Alamance, he would again find time to enjoy the civilized life of the town. He warned his troops that "the slightest insolence, or damage done to [the] town, would be severely punished." For most of the next week the community was full of soldiers, prisoners, and curiosity-seekers. Forty Regulators, bound two and two, were brought in the first day and thirty the next, and still others came on their own account, anxious to swear their allegiance to the crown and thereby win an executive pardon. The Brethren were now so much in the governor's trust that they were able to influence him favorably in his treatment of these men, not all of whom they felt deserved the reputation of lawbreakers. Even so, they were careful not to press the advantage. "Many came to Marshall and other Brethren begging for our good word, but we must move carefully in the matter, as we neither have nor dare claim such influence over His Excellency."[30]

On Thursday, the sixth of June, the whole town turned out to celebrate the birthday of the king. At ten that morning the people lining the street or standing at their windows could see the trombonists and violinists leading the governor and his troops in a spirited procession up from the creek bottom, and then on up through the center of town and out to a field where, for the next two hours or more, the soldiers marched and maneuvered grandly. By the middle of the afternoon the maneuvers were over and Tryon was seated comfortably in a huge tent that dominated the town square. Presently Brother

Marshall appeared in the door, and with him three other Moravian Brethren, including Traugott Bagge, all adopting a most solemn air as their leader read a proclamation expressing "the warmest Sentiments of Allegiance" to the crown. "At each mention of *His Majesty*, or *His Excellency*," the diarist tells us, "the four Brethren bowed profoundly." This somber mood soon lifted when the governor invited the Brethren to table. He and his guests drank each other's health with loud "Hurras" and a great sound of trombones while about them the afternoon drifted away "brightly and happily," the celebration finally drawing to a close late that evening in a sputtering flare of rockets set off in front of the governor's tent.[31]

And so it went through all of those pleasant spring days. When the time came for His Excellency's departure "his face showed as much emotion as though he were bidding farewell to his own family. The Governor wanted to pay for what had been furnished to him, but this was not allowed, and he accepted it as a token of regard for him, and gave most courteous thanks, and sent greetings to our whole Society."[32]

2

"My Name Shall Be There"

The success of Governor Tryon's expedition into the backcountry left the Moravian leaders free to proceed with what, after all, was their chief unfinished business in Wachovia, the building of their central town, Salem, the "city of peace." Bethabara, the "house of passage," would now revert to what it had been in the beginning, primarily an agricultural community, while Salem would become the seat of church government and a focal point for Moravian commercial enterprises, a town "not . . . for farmers but for those with trades."[1]

The search for a site had begun as early as 1759. But it was not until the middle of the next decade, after the termination of the Indian wars and the arrival of Frederic William Marshall, that the Brethren set to work in earnest. Even then there was much haggling and uncertainty, not because appropriate sites were lacking—the surveyor Christian Reuter had marked off more than half a dozen in the early weeks of 1765—but because none of them had won approval in the drawing of the lot.

In the Moravian communities of that day the rule of the lot was absolute—an infallible means for discerning divine purpose in all matters important to community life. Should the stranger W—— be allowed to live in our town? Should Brother G—— be readmitted to Holy Communion? Is this the time to submit Brother H——'s marriage proposal to Sister P——? The Elders would draw the answer from a wooden bowl. It might be "*Ja,*" "*Nein,*" or merely a blank, depending on which of three specially prepared wood-and-paper reeds proved to be the divine choice. The *"Ja"* or *"Nein"* would end all further discussion for the moment; the blank suggested that the question was either premature or improperly stated, or perhaps that it should not have been asked at all.

If the Brethren relied on the lot for solutions to a whole range of relatively uncomplicated problems, as was certainly the case, obviously they would not neglect to do so in a matter as important as the founding of a city. But we must not think that they were given to consulting the lot in the manner of men casually drawing straws, or in the offhand fashion of parlor mystics seeking advice from the Ouija board or the *I Ching*. First they eliminated as many of the proposed town sites as they could reasonably be expected to eliminate on their own, and only then, with great care and reverence, did they appeal to the lot. But for each of the sites that Reuter and his associates had suggested to the Elders the answer was either "no" or else the blank was drawn. And then on 14 February of that same year, when yet another site was proposed, this one on a hill overlooking the middle fork of Muddy Creek, the answer was "yes." The text for the day seemed to confirm the choice: "Let thine eye be opened toward this house night and day, even toward the place of which thou hast said: My name shall be there."

But even after all this there was still very little popular support for the idea of building a third town in Wachovia. (Bethania, the second, had been founded in 1759, partly by Moravians, and partly by refugees of the French and Indian War.) The reason was that Bethabara had now become a prosperous town in its own right, a favorite stopping-off place for long hunters, peddlers, itinerant preachers, and cattle drovers, for judges and law clerks on their way to court in Salisbury, and for military authorities who periodically turned the low-lying bottoms along what is now Mill Creek into a parade or muster ground. If business was good and the people content, why throw everything over and start afresh?

Even the Elders seemed of two minds about the project, at times inclined to move ahead, at other times inclined to drop the whole thing. Unable to come to a decision, they appealed to their governing board in Herrnhut. But the members of that

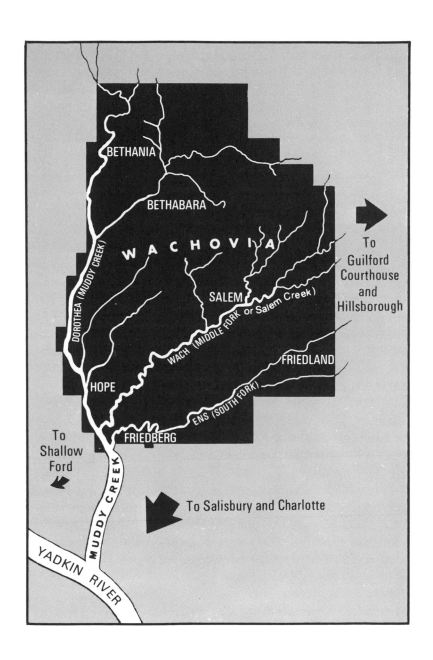

Wachovia in Revolutionary times

body had no final answers either and could only do what their brethren in America had already done: seek enlightenment through the lot. Was the building of Salem really an essential part of God's plan for Wachovia? The answer was an unqualified "yes." And so by return mail came word that the undertaking "had been positively ordered by the Saviour"[2] and would no longer admit of delay.

"Already. . . before we received these letters, we had faintheartedly made a small beginning there, but now in hope and faith we took up the work." And the work prospered even though it sometimes seemed that a whole host of invisible forces had risen up to prevent the town from getting built, "for over and over new ax-helves broke as though sawed in two, though no flaw in the wood could be discovered."[3]

For Traugott Bagge the long-awaited move to Salem took place on a bright springlike morning in January of 1772. Bagge set out for the new town with his wife Rachel, his two-year-old daughter Elisabeth, and four wagons piled high with store goods, household furnishings, and other belongings. In Bethabara, Bagge had been primarily a merchant and bookkeeper; in Salem, he would be much more: merchant, bookkeeper, political strategist, overseer of the town's financial affairs, public spokesman, unofficial purchasing agent for the American Revolutionary forces, and, in time, a legislator and justice of the peace.

Salem had about sixty inhabitants at the time of his arrival. Within another year it would have more than twice that many, still not a great figure by today's standards or even by the standards of that day, and yet impressive enough when we remember that the carpenters and brickmasons had been at work for only six years and that there were no real towns anywhere in the backcountry. At any rate there must have been many things about Salem to belie its lack of size. We see the town in these years as a place filled with the incessant noise of construction, the clang of broadax and blacksmith's hammer, the bustle of farm wagons, a great whirring of looms and spindles. "The present building of Salem is an extraordinary affair, which I would not have undertaken had not the Saviour

Himself ordered it," Brother Marshall had declared early in
1771. "I verily believe that the rich city of London could not do
that which we must accomplish—move the entire town and its
businesses to another place."[4]

Within another year Salem would completely outstrip the
older community, not only in point of size but also as a trade
center and oasis for thirsty travelers, and would soon (if it had
not already) overtake the busy court towns of Salisbury and
Hillsborough. By the end of 1774 it would definitely have
emerged as the leading commercial center of the entire
Piedmont and would have become essentially the town it was
to remain throughout the war years. To the wayfarer
coming upon it in the dusk of an autumn day and seeing far
below him the beckoning lights of Salem Tavern, the town must
already have seemed quite old, perhaps even a little
mysterious: the cluster of solidly built half-timbered structures,
some of brick, some of mud and wattle, with their
steeply pitched roofs, looming up quite unexpectedly out of
the Carolina wilderness, like a small-scale Heidelberg or
Düsseldorf, the houses situated not in typical pioneer fashion,
in the middle of vast yards carved out of seemingly
impenetrable forests, but more or less in a style characteristic of
Europe in medieval times. There seems to have been more side
yard than could be found in most parts of Europe, but the
whole was strikingly reminiscent of middle European towns,
the porch stoops and the houses themselves where there was
no stoop built squarely against the dirt streets. How much more
mysterious it might have seemed had this same wayfarer
ventured into town on that warm spring morning in 1769 when
the carpenters were just completing the framing for the Single
Brothers' choir house. On that day, the Salem diary tells us, the
musicians clambered up the walls and "blew their trumpets
from the top of the house."[5]

The building of a town devoted to industry and the
handicrafts could hardly have come at a more advantageous
time. The middle years of the eighteenth century were boom
times along the Carolina frontier. The rapid settlement of this
vast region brought with it an insatiable demand for ironwork,
cookware, leather products, and many other consumer goods.
In that day the Great Wagon Road out of Philadelphia was still

the most traveled route into the Carolina backcountry; and yet, despite its name, the road was in some places hardly more than a narrow winding trail, so that settlers moving south could bring only a fraction of the goods they would need in the new land. "Necessary items such as hand tools, bedding, and the like, could quickly fill a small Conestoga wagon; consequently the new Carolina settler was quick to look for local artisans who could produce household items that were needed after a house was raised. The Moravians were quick to answer that need."[6]

This was why Gottfried Aust's pottery so quickly became an institution in Salem. The potter himself, a tactless ill-tempered old fellow who kept sloppy books, abused his apprentices, and spoke out at all the wrong times against the new American government and its paper currency, nevertheless seems to have been an expert craftsman, capable of turning out a superior brand of queensware as well as the earthen jugs and serving bowls that were the staple of his business. During busy periods of trade, anxious customers frequently mobbed the place, and on at least one occasion things became so tense that Colonel Martin Armstrong, commanding officer of the Surry military district and self-appointed protector of the Moravians, had to drive the crowd back with his sword.

In the beginning the main emphasis in Wachovia had been on self-sufficiency—in itself an unusual thing in a region still bound by seemingly unbreakable commercial ties with England—but within a matter of months after the arrival of the first settlers trade was already brisk.

In the fall of 1754, when a gang of bloody whisky-soaked militiamen gathered for muster in a field near Bethabara and later began shooting up the town, the Wachovia diarist was moved first to anger and then to an understanding of the economic benefits: "We hope the soldiers will hereafter find another place for Muster, and not use our land. However, this time there was this much benefit—the neighboring people have found out that we have all sorts of things to sell, that we know exactly what we have, and that we will sell only for immediate payment."[7]

The outbreak of hostilities with England obviously created an even more acute demand for all kinds of products that were nowhere immediately available except in the stores at Salem and Bethabara. The Moravian wagons now shuttled with increased regularity between Wachovia and such trade centers as Cross Creek (Fayetteville), Petersburg, Virginia, and especially Charleston, South Carolina, exchanging deerskins, otter pelts, the fur of fox and raccoon, cornmeal, flour, tallow, wheat, flax, tobacco products, Seneca snakeroot, and other goods for indigo, salt, spices, pewter, raw iron, Negro slaves, rum, sugar, coffee, tea, and the hops needed for the production of "wholesome" Moravian beer.

On transferring their workshops and retail outlets to Salem the Brethren had abandoned the "pilgrim economy" or joint housekeeping that had been a subject of so much concern to Governor Tryon, though without abandoning its basic underlying principles. It was true that the tradesmen now worked more for themselves and less for the community, but they were still bound by strict rules. They could not change jobs or strike out on their own without the approval of town leaders, nor could a Brother dispose of his home or business except in ways that would prevent the "wrong sort" from getting hold of it.

The business of buying and selling lay principally with the church-owned community store. Located on what is now South Main Street, just across from Salem Square, and operated jointly with the store in Bethabara, this establishment was described by one postwar visitor as "the best country store in the United States."[8] Here Bagge gathered in skins and hides and other raw products of the backcountry against the day when he or one of his assistants would load up the wagons and set out for the markets in Cross Creek or Charleston. Both warehouse and retail outlet, the community store also served for many years as a home for Bagge and his family. There were other church-owned businesses in Salem, such as the pottery and the "red" tannery (which processed the heavier types of hides), and the men who operated these businesses were all men of considerable influence in the community; but in another sense they were no more independent than an ordinary wage earner or office manager in our own time. The price they could charge for their wares was fixed by town decree, as were their salaries and annual bonuses, and at no time could they branch out into areas of trade controlled by the Salem store. This, as upstart profiteers were often reminded, was "against the organization of the community." The town's newly "independent" craftsmen were also prohibited from selling their products except at a fixed price, and were as helpless as the lowliest hireling when it came to determining their own rate of pay. To this extent Salem offered them little they had not known in Bethabara. The big difference was that each man was now free to set up his own household, again within certain limits, and could decide for himself how to spend the money he received back from the congregation *Diaconie*[9] in the form of wages. In the old days that had been for the authorities to decide. It is plain to see that under either system the church exerted almost total control over both the means of an individual's livelihood and the fruits of his labor.

One of the most striking features of the Moravian economy was a European-style guild system under which boys of about fourteen were bound over to senior tradesmen for a seven-year apprenticeship. Or rather what was most striking was not so much the system itself as the rigid manner in which its rules were enforced. In some northern cities apprentices could become independent after only about three years of training; not so in Salem. The town Elders absolutely insisted that both parties to an agreement adhere to the terms of their contract. This emphasis on adequate preparation goes a long way toward explaining why the trademark "Made in Salem" came to stand for a particularly high order of quality workmanship. And there is no question whatsoever that the handiwork of these Salem craftsmen was the envy of the colony. This was brought home with great vividness in September of 1775 when a member of the Provincial Congress sought unsuccessfully to bar Wachovia's participation in an economic program under which bounties were to be paid as a means of stimulating home industry, his reason being that the Moravians "would win all the premiums."[10]

It was during these same years that church leaders set up a board of overseers, known as the *Aufseher Collegium*—Traugott Bagge, chairman—to regulate the trades, superintend financial arrangements, suppress unwelcome competition, and discipline craftsmen who repeatedly fell short of certain agreed-upon standards of conduct. Was a Brother slovenly in his work habits, reckless with his money, impudent to superiors? Whatever the answer, the *Collegium* was certain to look into the matter with extraordinary care; and in fact almost nothing likely to affect the economic or moral well-being of the community, either directly or indirectly, seems to have escaped this body's all-inquisitive eye.

Have the Brethren been indulging too freely in the brandy and drinking too little of our "wholesome" beer? Will Brother Charles Holder please explain why he refuses to pay his debts? Can nothing be done to bring Brother Yarrell's inventories to a proper accounting? Or to keep Brother Stockburger's blind horse out of the streets? Or to prevent the Single Brothers' celebrated jumping bull from trampling our gardens and fences? And what of the unsightly "gallows" Brother Aust has erected in front of his house? Can he not find a more suitable way to intimidate trespassers and deter stray cattle?

But soon now such questions would give way to far more momentous concerns.

3

For Boston or the King?

In May of 1775 Bishop John Michael Graff, Salem
minister and perceptive diarist, was still able to declare that
"our sky has remained clear in spite of the unrest in the land."
But this was the spring of Lexington, Concord, Ticonderoga,
Bunker Hill. And as the news of these battles spread through
the backcountry so did the unrest and violence and so did the
demand for the Moravians to declare themselves. Did they hold
with the king or with Boston? Their answer was invariably the
same: they would remain loyal to King George and would do
"all in our power to preserve freedom, so long as we are not
asked to do aught against our conscience, that under no
circumstances will we bear arms, or personally take part in
military service, though we will pay instead."[1]

The idea of professing loyalty to the king and in the same
breath espousing the cause of freedom may seem to us
contradictory and even a bit foolhardy. It was not that at all. At
the time the argument of colonial leaders was not so much with
the crown, or rather with the abstract rights of the crown, as
with Parliament, and it was still popular to stand up for the
king while denouncing his ministers. As long as this state of
affairs existed the Moravian Brethren were able to quote the
British law which had granted freedom of conscience, and also
the right not to bear arms, with some assurance that provincial
officers would heed their pleas of neutrality.

But it had now become more obvious that this would not
always work. As summer came on the fever of rebellion spread

even more rapidly through the backcountry. In Mecklenburg County disgruntled citizens had adopted a series of resolves branding royal authorities as little better than outlaws and choosing a committee of eighteen selectmen to take over the government of the county.

In June a Mecklenburg tavernkeeper, Captain James Jack, arrived in Salem by way of Philadelphia, where he had delivered to the Second Continental Congress a set of the resolves and, some believe, a copy of the county's legendary Declaration of Independence. Captain Jack's mission had been more symbolical than useful. Although the First Continental Congress had urged Americans to arm themselves and had proposed sweeping economic sanctions against England, the second was in a more conciliatory mood and would take no action on the resolves or on the Mecklenburg Declaration, if indeed there ever was such a document. Most historians doubt that there was: the only evidence was a statement written from memory some time after a May twentieth meeting in which the people of Mecklenburg were said to have declared themselves "a free and independent people."

Captain Jack had arrived in Salem with two other documents, both addressed to Traugott Bagge. One was a circular containing "an Encouragement to take up arms" and the other a proclamation urging the Brethren (and all other colonists) to set aside 20 July as "a Day of Fasting, Humiliation and Prayer." From his conversation with the Mecklenburg emissary Bagge must have sensed the growing mood of restlessness in the land. His comment that Captain Jack's home county had "declared itself free and *independent* of England, and made such arrangements for the administration of the laws among them as the Continental Congress later made for the whole country" comes as close as any other to proving the existence of the Mecklenburg Declaration, but might just as easily be taken to refer to the only slightly less radical resolves adopted on 31 May.[2]

All that summer and fall and on into the new year, militant patriots and sometimes loyalists as well rode into town and solicited Moravian support. For Boston or the king? The strategy of patriot leaders was to hold out to the Brethren the lure of political gain. This was why Bagge and Dr. Jacob Bonn were "especially invited" to join other Surry voters in an election to choose delegates to the Provincial Congress. Led by Bagge, the Brethren unfailingly spurned all such invitations, even though there was a sizable bloc of opinion that would have had them "serve if elected." Such was the counsel of the former Bethabara minister, John Ettwein, now a Tory-minded spokesman for the Moravian congregations in Pennsylvania. Despite his rigidly pacifist views, Ettwein believed that any Moravian who chose to serve as a provincial delegate or in any other capacity would be only fulfilling the responsibilities of citizenship, "and if the inhabitants trust one and elect him I think it would be wrong and dangerous to forbid him to accept."[3]

In retrospect, this appears to have been rather unsound advice, and was received with little favor even at the time. The Brethren could hardly have boasted of consistency or expected any real sympathy for their views if, at a later date, when the shooting war became more intense, they had been forced to explain away their membership on "freedom committees" while stoutly defending their right not to bear arms.

But the wisdom of this standoffish attitude may not have been immediately apparent to everyone. Their refusal to have anything to do with the Surry election did not diminish and may even have intensified efforts "to draw the Brethren into the game." Thus it was that Bagge and two other Moravians, Jacob Blum of Bethabara and George Hauser, Sr., of Bethania, found themselves appointed to the Surry County Committee of Safety. When they politely declined that honor, they were summoned before three representatives of the committee and invited to explain themselves further. Bagge offered much the same explanation that had been offered before: that they "could not take part in such discussions because the Brethren did not bear arms." The men retaliated by ordering Dr. Bonn, a justice of the peace and chairman of the county court, to issue no warrants for debt and, in effect, to cease all but the more superficial functions of his office.[4]

Prior to the conference Bagge had received from Joseph Williams, one of the delegates to the Hillsborough Congress and a man of some stature in local Revolutionary War annals, a special invitation to meet with "certain gentlemen from this county . . . to consider conditions in the land." Again he was forced to explain that this was out of the question, and yet in less than two weeks he received another invitation from the same delegate. This time he made no effort to reply. He was now convinced, however, that if anyone purporting to be a Moravian had appeared in Hillsborough he would immediately have been given "seat and vote" with no questions asked, on the presumption, of course, that he would not stoop so low as to vote the "Tory" line.[5]

Actually there was very little reason to assume anything of the kind. The usual presumption, seemingly borne out by the refusal of Moravian leaders to participate in such meetings, was just the opposite: that they were all actively sympathetic to the Tory, or loyalist, cause. Sympathetic they may have been; active they were not. It would have been well if in trying to get this message across—in trying to persuade the Whigs that they were not loyalists and the loyalists that they were not Whigs—they had been forced to deal only with the lies and complaints and arguments of their enemies. Unfortunately there was also the problem of how to stamp out dissension within their own congregations, particularly among the younger members, for whom the doctrine of noninvolvement seemed impractical and perhaps even cowardly in these heady times when everywhere was heard the cry of "Liberty!" Their willingness to express their whiggish sympathies openly, even as their Tory-minded parents were discreetly hiding their own, and to hold themselves available for armed service would later bring this lament from Bishop Graff: "This morning several men came from Capt. Schmidt's Company and took Lorenz Vogler away from here. There is reason to believe that he was party to the plan, for he went with them willingly. On the contrary Philipp Hill positively refused, and they desisted from their efforts with him. Like Vogler, there have been three young men taken from Bethania, George and John Hauser, and Samuel Strub; they are entirely worldly minded."[6]

One could forgive these young men much even if their elders and the church authorities had all been able to agree that the bearing of arms was morally wrong everywhere and in all circumstances. The truth is that there had never been any such agreement. What they did agree on, in this particular instance, was the need for neutrality, but this need derived at least in part from grounds other than strict pacifist convictions.

This does not mean that the pacifists among them could not find ample doctrinal support for their views. Ever since the time of Peter of Chelcicky, a fifteenth-century Bohemian monk who opposed bloodshed in whatever form and on whatever pretext, the Unity of Brethren had held to the idea of pacifism as a desirable norm if not as an outright article of faith. To put it another way: pacifism as practiced by the Unity was something entirely different from pacifism as practiced by the Quakers, whose New Garden Meeting was founded about the same time as Bethabara. For these Quakers, as for the early followers of Peter of Chelcicky, the Biblical admonition "Thou shalt not kill" was to be taken literally. This, however, was a view that had never prevailed among a majority of Moravians at any time since the revival of the church in the early eighteenth century. Even the Reverend Mr. Ettwein, the most fervent pacifist of the time, was always careful to distinguish between pacifism as a philosophy and pacifism as "a point of doctrine."[7]

Some years after the war he was to tell Alexander Hamilton that members of his church had traditionally "agreed to make one of their principles or rules not to fight with carnal weapons but with prayer." One was not to assume, on the other hand, "that each and every member belonging to the Moravian Church has such scruples of conscience. A soldier could become and remain a member."[8]

Many, in fact, already had. Wasn't it a matter of record that any number of Moravian colonists had borne arms during the Indian wars? The question was often to haunt church leaders during the Revolutionary years. This was true even though many of them, Ettwein included, believed that under the conditions of frontier life it was often acceptable to shoot Indians, robbers, murderers, or wild animals "since none of these recognize or are subject to any regulation or authority."[9] The sin came when one attempted to defend himself against duly constituted authority, as American patriots were doing, or took up arms in his own behalf when such authority already existed for his protection.

With Ettwein, then, as with other Moravian leaders, the key argument for noninvolvement was not the Sixth Commandment but Romans 13: "Let every soul be subject to the higher powers. For there is no power but of God; the powers that be are ordained of God." Again: "Render therefore to all their dues: tribute to whom tribute is due; custom to whom custom; fear to whom fear; honor to whom honor."

This explains why Moravians were willing to do "whatever was required" in order to enjoy their exemption from military service, why they agreed to pay without complaint the threefold tax imposed on them in 1779. The Quakers, by contrast, seem never to have paid these taxes at any time during the war; they were fined instead. Furthermore, they repudiated such "fighting Quakers" as General Nathanael Greene and even the erratic Hermon Husbands, who wasn't much of a soldier but who had advocated violence, or at least had not opposed it, as a means of correcting the abuses that led up to the Battle of Alamance.

Unquestionably there were many Moravians who felt as strongly as the Quakers about the horrors of bloodshed, who still clung with unwavering conviction to a literal interpretation of the scriptural doctrine of pacifism. But the church stopped short of formally repudiating members who chose to go to war or sit on Revolutionary committees. Even in Wachovia, where there was an overriding and even a desperate need for unity, the military-minded were never censured for their conduct— not in the sense, say, that they would have been censured for violating some aspect of the community's moral code. Ettwein, who continued to correspond with the Wachovia congregations and they with him long after he had returned to Pennsylvania, consistently urged the Brethren to deal with such matters in an evenhanded manner. As for himself, he would remain loyal to the crown until "the event should prove that God Himself had severed America from England." And he never compromised on this point. He remained a pacifist (and a Tory) right up till the end of the war when he too became persuaded "that allegiance to the new republic represented his religious duty."[10]

Ettwein also put forward a more practical basis for Moravian neutrality: the fear that if members of the church did take up arms against the king the interest of their brethren in England and other countries would suffer. As the scholar and archivist

Dr. Adelaide Fries was to put it more than a century later, the Moravians remembered "that they were members of a worldwide Unity and that if they formally renounced allegiance to Great Britain it could be used to the detriment of their Brethren living in England and in the British West Indies; moreover, changes in the field of service were quite usual among them, and they hesitated to erect a barrier between American and English congregations."[11]

Their uncommitted status served other tactical advantages as well. What better way, for example, to secure their land against the not unlikely possibility of a British victory? It must have caused them a great deal of uneasiness to know that they did not really own that land outright, that it was still technically British property. As members of an unincorporated religious body, the Brethren had been unable to take title directly. The man chosen as principal trustee was a London bookseller named James Hutton. Hutton, one of the chief officers of the Unity in Great Britain, had agreed to hold the land "for the Use, Benefit and Behoof of the said *Unitas Fratrum*."[12] Only a legal technicality, to be sure. Still, the Brethren had good reason to worry about what a London lawyer might do with that clause if they were to become too active in the struggle for independence. All that aside, they did not want to take a chance on losing the religious and political advantages which they and they alone shared with the Church of England.

As Dr. Fries says, "Few of them were of English birth, yet they could claim privileges accorded to no English born 'Dissenters,' but granted to the Brethren by Act of Parliament, and for this they were grateful, and for this they felt under obligations to the English Crown."[13]

The manner in which they came by these privileges is an interesting story in itself. The Moravians had originally sought exemption from military service and the swearing of public oaths as part of the religious freedom they had hoped to find, but had not found, in the New World. They had never been tortured or hanged for their beliefs, as the Quakers had in an earlier time, but there had been many serious annoyances and some persecution, especially along the New York frontier. Influenced by liquor dealers who feared that the spread of the Herrnhut gospel was cutting into their trade with the Indians, authorities in that province enacted a harsh licensing act against the Moravians and other "vagrant preachers . . . or disguised Papists"[14] and finally slapped two of their missionaries in jail for refusing to swear an oath of loyalty to King George.

This, together with reports of similar incidents in England, persuaded the Moravian leader Count Zinzendorf that London might now respond favorably to an appeal for relief. But Zinzendorf and his allies wanted more than just relief, more than just the right not to be harrassed by colonial functionaries. They wanted an act that would free the Moravians from what has been described as "the stigma of disloyalty and sectarianism"[15] and gain for them nothing less than the same legal standing enjoyed by the Church of England.

Many authorities must have found it strange that an evangelical folk practicing a kind of primitive communism and preaching a gospel of salvation-by-faith hardly distinguishable from Anabaptist doctrine would even aspire to so elevated a status. Hadn't the unorthodox Methodist reformer John Wesley borrowed heavily from these Moravians, and weren't they everywhere known for their compassion and humility and other unchurchly traits? All true. Like Wesley, however, the Moravians protested that they were not Dissenters and had therefore been unfairly denied their legal rights. That they were disconcertingly pious in an age of reason and classical learning did not mean that they had no respect for form and ritual, no love for the ancient mysteries of their faith, no reverence for the hallowedness of festal days and sacred places. For the purposes of the Moravian lobbying effort in Parliament the main point of all this was that they had preserved intact this episcopal tradition through more than three centuries of dispersion and persecution. They could trace their beginnings back to the fifteenth-century Bohemian martyr John Hus, and through him and his followers all the way back to the first apostles. Wasn't this proof enough that the Moravian bishops stood fully in the line of apostolic succession?

Somehow Zinzendorf and his lobbyists managed to put this argument across. Impressed by their thorough documentation of the church's position, assured that "its doctrine was pure and its discipline correct,"[16] and encouraged furthermore in the belief that recognition of a truly "apostolic people" would benefit Anglican officials in America, where there was little sympathy for bishops, sacraments, and obscure liturgies, Parliament at length voted into law a bill upholding the validity of Zinzendorf's petition and allowing him and the other leaders of the Unity to turn a new face to the world.

This was the act under which the Unity became known as an "ancient Protestant Episcopal Church"—a designation valuable on several counts, first off because it permitted the Brethren to refuse military induction without going to jail and to affirm rather than swear their public oaths, and also because it provided the basis for a 1755 North Carolina law that allowed them to set up and support their own parish government, a right denied to all other non-Anglican settlers. We can be sure that this privileged status won them no friends among competing religious groups. It was, in fact, as we have already seen, a source of some discord during the Regulator years. In like manner we can more easily understand why they clung so adamantly to their neutralist position right on up to the time English law was no longer recognized in the colonies, and indeed kept on clinging to it long after that.

In the summer and fall of 1775 the Moravians had only begun not to fight. Previously, they had been able to argue their case in an atmosphere not yet colored by the fanaticism and bitterness of total war. But for the next six years or more there would be no letup in the assault on their claim to special parliamentary immunities, little or no letup in the impatient and inquisitorial demands of militia officers and zealous patriots, practically all of whom seemed to believe that if the Brethren could not be forced to bear arms they could at least be forced to give up the products of their plantations and workshops to the cause of liberty, which, of course, they would have consented to do without all the disruption and violence. If the Quakers suffered less during these years, the reason may be that they had settled on random farms, had created no towns, and offered few worldly comforts to attract the eye of a piratical and half-starved soldiery.

The contrast between these Quaker settlements and the new town of Salem must have been quite remarkable. The contrast was not less great between Salem and most of the other towns in the backcountry. In Salem as nowhere else there already existed an embryo of the new industrial order, a way of thinking common to the late nineteenth century but altogether rare during the colonial and Revolutionary era. In an almost unimaginably brief space of time these Moravian tradesmen had created a sophisticated economy and social system highly dependent on balanced budgets, expert craftsmanship, efficient marketing, and far-flung trade routes, a society that for all of these reasons and perhaps others was exceedingly vulnerable to the crosscurrents of revolution. It seems almost too obvious to say—and yet it is necessary to say—that prosperity had become in many ways their most deadly enemy. "To Salem" became the cry of every pressman or captain-of-the-day bent on procuring beef or brandy for his militia unit and of every liberty man or backwoods peddler anxious to dump his rapidly depreciating paper currency. Many of these people bought all they could, stole some more, and then murmured that the Moravians must be secretly in league with Great Britain and "must be getting goods from there."[17] If not, why did they seem so prosperous when everybody else was in the throes of want?

To allay such suspicions and to protect themselves against wholesale depredations (and also to slow the rapid influx of paper money) Moravian business leaders took the extraordinary step of voluntarily reducing their retail stocks at a time when merchants in neighboring communities had sold out of everything and had no prospect of getting more. The Elders Conference had "consulted the Saviour about the matter, and received the good and necessary advice that we should reduce our stock of goods as much as possible."[18] It was in the same spirit that they had turned down an opportunity to establish a retail outlet in the growing market town of Cross Creek.

They also began urging the townspeople to keep their muskets out of sight "since we have conscientious scruples against bearing arms"[19] and voted to place under lock and key the gunpowder they had kept on hand for defensive purposes. But nothing much seemed to help. Suspicions that they were not really pacifists but undercover agents for the British crown persisted till the last days of the war. And so did the demand for booty: beef, cornmeal, bread, shoes, draught horses, oxen, oats by the bushel and wagonload, lead for bullets, livestock, leather jackets, buckskin breeches, fine linenwear, and good Moravian brandy.

Sometimes these demands were accompanied by "tickets" which theoretically gave the Moravians a monetary claim against the state, but which apparently were never redeemed for more than a fraction of their value—if that. Nor would the lack of such tickets prevent the more irresponsible officers and enlisted men from roaming and looting at will. "The poor men must and will make war," Bishop Graff observed, "but have none of those things that are necessary."[20]

4

The Liberty Men

In the days to come great crowds of these liberty men appeared on the streets of the Moravian towns, men dressed not in the usual military issue but in moccasins and hunting shirts and leather knee breeches, the only "uniform" widely available at the time, some of them carrying longrifles and muskets or old fowling pieces, and wearing bucktails in their hats to show "they are for freedom."[1] With them came an almost constant flood of rumors. There were reports that the king's standard had been raised at Cross Creek, that the royal governor-in-exile Josiah Martin had landed at Wilmington with hundreds of British troops, that former Governor Tryon had also landed, or would soon land, and, as always, that the Moravians had been secretly aiding the loyalist cause. There was even a report to the effect that Governor Martin had been hiding out in Salem ever since his escape from the New Bern palace. None of this was true, but all of it hinted at new trouble for these quiet villagers.

On the night of 4 December 1775 the skies of Wachovia lit up with an awesome display of meteor showers, an omen perhaps of what the new year was to bring, for now almost daily there were desperate men in the streets, men stirred up by rumor and fear and reacting to both in the only way they knew how—by threatening to execute the Moravians and put their towns to the torch.

There must have been many times during these early weeks of 1776 when the more logical course for the Brethren would have been to settle such matters with their fists, or with bludgeons outside in the snowy dark. They seem never to have succumbed to that temptation and, what is the more remarkable, usually managed to stay out of the heated political quarrels that sprang up in their midst. When the Baptist preacher and fierce patriot William Hill fell to arguing with a royalist one night in the tavern at Bethabara, a bystander explained: "If Mr. Hill expresses his opinion concerning the present circumstances it is only said 'Mr. Hill says so and so'; but if one us said anything at once it was reported 'the *Moravians* say thus and so'; and so we say nothing about the matter!"[2]

Of all the rumors, the most persistent was that Governor Martin had returned in triumph from his offshore exile. The governor, under constant surveillance by the New Bern Committee of Safety, had fled the colony in the spring of 1775, seeking refuge first at Fort Johnston in the mouth of the Cape Fear and later fleeing to a British warship outside the Wilmington harbor. For weeks prior to his departure his counsels had gone unheeded and his proclamations scorned. When he summoned the rebellious legislature to meet in New Bern on 4 April, having persuaded himself that his words still commanded respect, members promptly united behind House Speaker John Harvey and met on 3 April in the same town—not as a legislature but as a revolutionary assembly, the purpose of which was to pass anti-British resolutions and elect delegates to the Second Continental Congress. So Martin had no choice but to flee. One pictures him in an almost frantic attitude of running, hurriedly spiking the palace cannon, burying his ammunition in a cabbage patch, and then fleeing in great wild haste from "the monster sedition." But he was no coward. In the waning days of royal authority he had openly denounced the revolutionary leaders and the violence done by their "little, unrestrained and arbitrary Tribunals" and had attempted to thwart their designs with every means at his disposal. And that was still his chief aim during the long months he was to spend aboard the British ship *Cruizer*. He had developed highly elaborate and even tedious plans for the conquest of the province, and had repeatedly petitioned the

British high command for the arms and men necessary to put them into effect.[3]

Though 1776 dawned with Martin still futilely pacing the floor of his cabin, the prospects for an invasion were anything but remote. This was all the more true now that civil war had erupted between the liberty men and the newly aroused Tories, who had much claim on the sentiment of the colony, if not on its political machinery, and who could be expected to rise in even greater numbers if the British were actually to effect a landing.

On 6 March the one-handed peddler and Tory cavalryman Joseph Hughs, returning from Cross Creek where he had been briefly held prisoner, reported that the Whig and Tory armies had clashed in a savage battle at Moores Creek Bridge, a wilderness crossing some eighteen miles north of Wilmington. For weeks the news of this impending conflict had been the talk of street corner and tavern, and the Moravians had watched with growing consternation as first the liberty men and then whole companies of former Regulators, who, ironically, had remained loyal to the king, flooded into their towns. These men had suffered such wholesale indignities in Governor Tryon's time that many of them seemed more interested in revenging themselves on the eastern militia leaders who had helped smash the Regulator rebellion than in joining other colonists in the struggle for independence. But they were again without competent leadership or adequate weapons, neither of which was to be found when they reached their rendezvous point some sixty miles south of Salem. Here they had expected to make contact with a large detachment of British troops. Instead, they found only an impeccably attired Scottish officer, Captain Donald McLeod, who had been sent to escort them to Cross Creek, and a hosghead of rum "which most of them visited industriously."[4] The rum gone and someone having spread the word that a party of Whigs was marching against them, these rambunctious backwoodsmen suddenly flung off in all directions, like a flock of besotted geese, leaving Captain McLeod, for whom they had no small amount of contempt anyway, to find his own way out of the wilderness. They would not go far, most of them, because they no longer had anywhere to go; many of these men, these "outlyers," as they had come

The Tories found only an impeccably attired Scottish officer and a hogshead of rum "which most of them visited industriously"

to be called, were so well known for their royalist sentiments that they could not have remained safely on their farms even if they had chosen to return.

"The few that passed through Salem returned much depressed, and without having had part in the frolic,"[5] Bagge said.

Others may have recovered from their fright in time to join crown forces at Moores Creek Bridge. If so, they were very much in the minority—then and later. Despite the brisk stir they made in the Moravian towns and despite what was believed in the backcountry for many years, the Regulators were not all to become active Tories, or even Tory sympathizers; and certainly at this point did not figure significantly in the fight to restore royal rule. For this the governor and his council of war had to depend almost exclusively on a huge contingent of Scottish Highlanders, most of them recent immigrants who had settled in the Cape Fear region and who were grateful for the land grants they had won in exchange for their expressions of loyalty to the crown. In late February these men marched east with a wail of bagpipes and loud cries of "King George and broad swords!" hoping to reach the coast in time for a rendezvous with seaborne troops under General Henry Clinton.

But first there was Moores Creek Bridge. The Whigs won the race to that crossing. They got there late in the afternoon of 26 February, in time to strip most of the planking from the bridge and to grease the log sleepers with soap and tallow. All that night they waited amid shallow trenches and hastily raised breastworks. And then as dawn was coming on, and a mist beginning to creep up from the swamp, they could see the highlanders coming, their weapons glinting in the eerie half-light, the air again filled with shouts of "King George and broad swords!" and a lively wail of bagpipes. And then filled with something else: the boom of patriot artillery fire and a pelting whine of bullets and swanshot. It was over in no more than three minutes, with most of the advance guard of the loyalist force, including the able if impetuous Captain McLeod, lying dead in the fetid backwater. What might have happened if the Highlanders had won the race and succeeded in joining forces with the British has been a matter of much speculation.

The actual result was that there was no invasion of North Carolina or even an attempt at invasion for another four and one-half years.

The Moravians meantime had fallen under the increasingly watchful eye of such patriot leaders as Richard Caswell, the commanding officer at Moores Creek Bridge. Some weeks before the actual fighting, Christian Heckewalder, the assistant storekeeper in Salem, had aroused the suspicion of American commanders while on a shopping expedition to Cross Creek, which was then in the hands of the loyalists. Caswell learned of the affair from a subordinate, who concluded that Heckewalder and his teamsters had gone to Cross Creek "under the Cloak of getting Salt"[6] when what they were really after was ammunition that could be put in safekeeping for the governor and his troops.

The Tories seemed equally suspicious of Moravian aims. As Brother Heckewalder was returning to Salem, a crowd of these men surrounded his wagons and "with many curses threatened to empty the salt on the ground and ruin it rather than let it be used by the *Rebels*."[7] Miraculously, Heckewalder was able to resume his journey the next day, his cargo of salt and other goods still intact.

The Salisbury Committee of Safety, one of six ad hoc councils set up to rule the province, had also learned of Heckewalder's "suspicious" behavior, and in less than two weeks after the return of the wagons a delegation of army officers came knocking at the doors of the Moravian towns. There were four members of the group, three militia captains and the always sympathetic Colonel Martin Armstrong, plus great numbers of enlisted men who stood around with guns loaded, "apparently waiting impatiently for the order to plunder." [8] Was it true, the delegation wanted to know, that the Moravians had been storing arms for the governor? Was it also true that they had consistently refused to accept the new paper currency as fair payment for their goods?

Bagge, the Moravian spokesman, explained as he had so many times before that it was "quite contrary" to their calling "to mix in political matters" and that, to make a long story short, no, they were not storing arms for the governor or for anyone else. To explain away their skepticism about the paper currency must have been much more difficult. Outspoken tradesmen such as the potter Aust had not even attempted to hide their feelings about the money, and not long before a visitor in Bethabara had become quite "wild and positive" over tavernkeeper Fockel's refusal to accept the stuff.[9]

And yet even this must have been explained to everyone's satisfaction, for now we see them, these men, not all of them by any means sympathetic to the Moravian position, sitting nodding politely and perhaps exchanging the ordinary pleasantries of the day, while all the others, the ones who had come to plunder, stood nervously fingering their rifles and growing perceptibly more disappointed at the lack of any encouraging sign from their leaders.

But it was not over yet. Reassured by Bagge's conciliatory manner, the delegation produced a copy of the test oath recently approved by the Provincial Congress. Would the Moravians sign? Unfortunately, no. Then what evidence did they have that they were not secretly aiding the king? Bagge provided that evidence in the form of a written declaration conceived on the spot and carefully hedged to say no more than he and the other leaders felt themselves obligated to say. In it they again pledged to demean themselves as a "quiet people," to refrain from all forms of political activity, to "cheerfully assist and support the Country along with our other fellow Inhabitants in paying of Taxes and anything else that is not against our Conscience & the Privileges upon which we have settled here" and to do nothing "that shall be detrimental to the good Province we inhabit."[10]

Later on this would not be good enough. Later they would be called upon for a more specific commitment to the cause of liberty. But on this amicable occasion the statement was accepted without question. Colonel Armstrong, most of all, seemed to find the Moravian response in every way satisfactory. Armstrong had consistently upheld the right of the Moravian settlers to remain neutral, and not only that but to be free as well of the harrassment and brutality which were too often their lot. In the Moravian diaries one often finds notations to the effect that "Col. Armstrong was here and was very friendly."[11] Many was the time that one of his "advertisements" meant the difference between an orderly encampment and a wholesale riot. Perhaps he understood what others sometimes did not understand: that the industrious Moravians could better serve the cause of independence by supplying the American armies with essential articles of war than by bearing arms. Or were his motives only those of a politically ambitious soldier and landowner who did not want to alienate so large a bloc of public support?

Whatever the answer, the Moravians had no real reason to expect his protection, and in fact they had not always held the colonel in such high esteem. In Regulator times, when both he and a rival landowner named Gideon Wright had been active in behalf of the crown, the Bethabara diarist had voiced a less than complimentary view of Armstrong's performance, observing that Wright "had shown more loyalty and courage than Armstrong, and had become a Colonel while Armstrong was only a Captain."[12]

The two men had actively supported the move to divide Rowan County, mainly because, as the diarist had long suspected, each wanted the new Surry courthouse for his own land. Wright won that battle, possibly as a result of his superior record in the War of the Regulation, but he did not long enjoy the advantage. In 1773, when the new county's southern boundary was shifted from a point just north of Salem to what is now the boundary between Forsyth and Davidson counties, land belonging to Armstrong and his brother was chosen as the more accessible site. The town built on that site—the "Old Richmond" of our day—was to serve as the seat of government until 1789, when the county was again divided. Armstrong and Wright had kept up a hostile and unbroken rivalry throughout this period, or rather until the latter's death late in 1782, and to a very great extent the story of the war in the backcountry can be found in the story of these men. Both were landowners of more than ordinary reputation, with extensive holdings on or near the Yadkin; both had held political office and military commissions; both had been shaped by similar backgrounds; and each had tried to have the other thrown in jail for the duration. But why, one wonders, would men with such similar interests and backgrounds now join opposing sides in a war in which the main point at issue was so sharply drawn? Was it out of deep-seated philosophical convictions, the hope of personal gain, or a combination of the two? If we could explain all this we might also be able to explain why hundreds of other backcountry settlers, many of them also shaped by an identical religious and economic background, some of them active in the Regulator rebellion and some not, also chose to fight on opposing sides—why this "Tory war" raged with such fury all up and down the Yadkin valley, with a fury said to have been unmatched anywhere else in the American colonies.

All that can be said with reasonable certainty is that by 1776 Armstrong had become a friend and protector of the Moravians and that any doubts they may once have had about his integrity, or courage, or selflessness, were now forgotten. "We may thank God," Bagge wrote, "that a man like Col. Martin Armstrong was and remained chief officer of Surry County throughout the war, for while sometimes need forced him to order, or have ordered, from us articles which were a loss to us, yet in general it was in his heart to make things as convenient as possible for us."[13]

But the help he sought to provide was not always readily available. By the early spring of 1776 the Wachovia settlements were again swarming with liberty men looking for a wild time and plenty of loot. From what Joseph Williams had said on 6 May, after returning from a meeting of the Provincial Congress in Halifax, the Moravians had thought they would be temporarily exempt from military duty. But the next day there came an ominous report that Heinrich Schmidt, the Bethania blacksmith who had recently been chosen militia captain for the Wachovia district, would meet with all "taxables" from Friedberg and certain other outlying Moravian settlements. These men assembled at Steiner's Mill, near Salem, and learned that their sons had been summarily inducted into Schmidt's company. There is no way of knowing how many of these young men were actually forced to serve, or for that matter how many chose to serve on their own accord; but as they were beginning to learn, they were not nearly as secure on their farms as they would have been in the closely knit congregation towns of Salem and Bethabara, and some occasionally sought refuge there.

Two days after Schmidt's forced muster, the Salem Brethren learned that four other Friedbergers, whose homes happened to lie south of the Surry County line, had been forcibly inducted into a Rowan company. Outraged by such presumption, two of their parents, Adam Spach and George Hartman, quickly took horse and rode to Salisbury to plead for an exemption. They succeeded in getting a temporary delay from the committee of safety, but were warned that they could not expect similar treatment on the next occasion.

The next occasion was not long in coming. Later that spring General Griffith Rutherford's impending campaign against the Cherokees, now allied with the British, was the talk of all Wachovia; and this time the Brethren would be expected to furnish their quota of men. Rutherford was later to win much acclaim for his march into Indian country. His 2,400-man army destroyed dozens of Cherokee villages and forced the Indians to cede all of their lands east of the Blue Ridge, as well as a large portion of their territory beyond the mountains. Of the young Moravians lured into this campaign, none were from Bethabara; and only two, Philipp Hill, who had at first refused to march, and Lorenz Vogler were from Salem. In both of these communities allegiance to pacifist-minded church leaders remained relatively durable throughout the war. But even here the threat of induction was always present. Sometimes when the visiting militia captains and their subordinates were not busy requisitioning supplies or frantically seeking to compel the Brethren's attendance at muster, they would knock on the doors of the houses and rudely insist that the dwellers sign the test oath. Or, in another mood, they might gather in small groups in front of the Salem *Gemein Haus*,[14] where the Sisters lodged, and just stand there in the hope that the young women would give them some encouragement. So far as is known, none did.

And then in early summer came a disturbance "the like of which probably never happened before in a Congregation Town." It was 22 June, Communion Day, when four army deserters filled with "godless and murderous intentions" rode into town. The men stocked up on booze, asked a lot of "impertinent" questions, "loaded their guns heavily," and then advanced on Salem Tavern like sansculottes against the Bastille. They rode their horses into the front hall and immediately assaulted Brother George Frey, a visitor from

Friedberg. The men slammed him to the floor and, holding him by the throat, worked him over with their gun barrels. His face and head bleeding, he finally wrestled free and made it safely out the back way. But during the next month his neighbors in Friedberg noticed that he had begun to act strangely, sometimes grabbing his gun and shouting wildly, "I must go; I am a liberty man!"[15]

After Frey's escape the desperados set upon the tavern-keeper Jacob Meyer and his wife. They hacked their way through locked doors, smashed the dinner table, stomped the baby's cradle, "from which the baby had just been lifted," attacked Brother and Sister Meyer with tomahawks, and then drove off a party of Single Brethren that had come on a peacemaking mission. Outside once more, they violently accosted three passersby, leaving one of them flattened in the dust, and again gave chase to the would-be peacemakers, throwing stones at the ones who had taken refuge in a dwelling next door to the tavern and pursuing the others to the Brothers House. They broke open the door, smashed windows, kicked and stomped on Brother Heinzmann the housefather, and then "beat about them with guns, tomahawks and clubs and a pair of fire tongs," smashing more windows and doors and critically wounding five lodgers, including Brother Heinzmann, before another party of Single Brethren strongarmed them into submission.[16]

The next morning, a bit more sober but hardly more penitent, they were carried away bound hand and foot to Richmond town. Brought back to stand trial before three justices of the peace, the men "lied persistently" in spite of the staggering array of evidence against them, but at last were forced to admit that "they had sworn to destroy the Brothers House and then the entire town." They were assessed a twenty-pound fine, for which they were given a proper receipt, and were then marched away under a heavy guard to the Salisbury jail. The Brethren had borne all this with their usual forbearance and understanding, except that from now on even the most pacifist-minded among them would feel some necessity for keeping "a good club within reach."[17]

Earlier that month Brother Bagge had witnessed the important battle at Fort Moultrie, South Carolina, a battle which resulted in heavy losses for the British and delayed further military activities in the Charleston area for more than two years. Bagge had gone to Charleston to procure goods for the community store and had been supervising the loading of his wagons when the approach of the British threw the town into turmoil. Overnight, the self-assured Charlestonians had become frightened refugees, fleeing the town with their slaves and with as many of their personal effects as could be gathered up in haste. Bagge's wagons were loaded and he himself ready to begin the long trek back to Salem when there came an order that no one was to leave without a permit from the American commander. The merchant procured a permit for himself and one of his teamsters, and by nightfall was ten miles west of the city. The next day, at a tavern, he made the acquaintance of a German farmer from one of the Congaree River settlements. The man was quite beside himself. He too had been trapped in the city and had gained his release only after promising to deliver a letter from the South Carolina governor to the Committee of Safety in Salisbury.

"The poor man preferred to go home, and let some one else carry out his commission, so Br. Bagge quietly took charge of the letter, and on the way back he delivered it to the Committee in Salisbury; and so he reached home safely."[18]

5

A Rain of Freedom

Toward the end of July Bishop Graff and some of the other Moravian leaders read a startling report in a Virginia newspaper. It seemed that the churches in that province had now dropped from their public litanies all references to King George and his family and had substituted a prayer *"For the Magistrates of the Commonwealth."*

"This would indicate that *Independence* has already been declared," the bishop wrote. "May God have mercy on us!"[1]

There was no official confirmation of the news until the afternoon of 6 August, when an American militia captain, accompanied by a caravan of packhorses and dirty soldiers, appeared in the drought-stricken town of Salem and posted on the tavern a notice "in which the Independence of the twelve [*sic*] United Provinces from the King of England was openly declared."[2]

The bishop responded to this notice only as one deeply in love with tradition and old ties could respond: "We sighed in our hearts, but the Text for today comforted us: 'For a small moment have I forsaken thee, but with great mercies will I gather thee.' "[3]

Soon now the Brethren would be almost wholly preoccupied with the problems of independence. Of more concern at the moment, however, was the prolonged drought. After almost a month without rain the vegetable patches and cornfields had wilted, and the sun bore down ever more oppressively out of the August haze. One evening some clouds had come up, and the crash of thunder had drowned out the *Singstunde*. But there was no rain—and still no rain during all of that hot becalmed week prior to the posting of the Declaration of Independence.

In Bethabara the news attracted even less attention, the diarist in that town remarking only that William Sheppard, the Surry militia officer and freedom delegate, had returned from a meeting of the Salisbury Committee of Safety "and brought with him a Declaration, dated July 4th, Philadelphia, which announced Independence, and related to various other things."[4]

Even if independence posed no immediate threat to the Moravian congregations the Brethren were not unaware of what it could mean to their future security. Thus were members of the Salem congregation "reminded that in these critical times they should be very careful of word and deed, and especially that they should not express an opinion before strangers, still less declare themselves for either side, and that if asked any questions on political matters they should excuse themselves from answering on the ground of ignorance."[5]

But the heavens seemed to speak an end to their fears. The next morning there was a good hard rain that was both a relief to the parched earth and a fulfillment of their daily text: "I will open rivers in high places, and fountains in the midst of valleys; I will make the dry land springs of water."

Within a matter of days the Salem Elders had taken the precaution of striking the king's name from their own litanies. Though many of these men obviously sympathized with Bishop Graff, and would have preferred to retain closer ties with England, they were quick to remember and apply the dictum of Romans 13: "Let every soul be subject to the higher powers." But in expressing their willingness to obey these powers—that is, the Whigs who controlled the new state government—the Moravians by no means relinquished claim to their traditional political and religious rights, rights tacitly recognized by the 1776 Provincial Congress though not as yet by its successor, the North Carolina General Assembly.

A year and a half after the posting of the Declaration the Brethren were still insisting that they would in no wise take up arms, but would willingly bear their share "of the burden of the land in these disturbed times if reasonable demands are made."

The militiamen posted on the tavern a notice in which American independence "was openly declared"

This time, however, they would find little reassurance in their daily text: "Peace be within thy walls," because there would be no real peace for many months and even years to come. The reason was not so much the aggressions of the British as the Tory-Whig schism that had ripped apart the political fabric of the state. "Just now the so-called Tories and Liberty Men are very hot against each other," Bishop Graff reported. And yet it was not really so much that the Tories and Whigs were at each other's throats, and forever making a ruckus in the Moravian towns, as that every profession of neutrality on the part of the Brethren was interpreted, at least by the more fanatical patriots, as merely an expression of sympathy for the king. Nor was that the whole story either: for though Loyalist sentiment ran high in many parts of the state, there were few places more infected by it than the upper Piedmont, and Surry County in particular, so that even though the British themselves might remain far from the scene there could be no peace or even an interlude that might be mistaken for peace until the last of the Tories and their sympathizers had been shackled, shot, or driven into exile.[6]

The result of all this was that the more perceptive Moravian leaders stubbornly sought to hold themselves aloof from the struggle. But to have done so would have required more than was either possible or desirable. It would have required them, first of all, to close down all of their shops, and stores, and taverns for the duration of the war. Only in this way, only by dismantling their entire economic system and becoming farmers, could they hope to keep the liberty men out of their settlements and themselves out of the thick of the revolutionary ferment.

By the time the real fighting began, the Brethren had won a just and widespread reputation for both the quality of their wares and the comforts of their inns. They had often entertained some of the leading men in the colony, and even now they would manage to preserve their civility, their sense of decorum, in spite of every threat. This does not mean that their towns could be judged by the standards of eighteenth-century British society, or that we must think of the Salem Tavern as a kind of swank London coffeehouse where insouciant poets, fashionably dressed dilettantes, and peri-wigged men of affairs could gather for temperate discussions of

Pope's couplets or Cromwell's politics. In these terrible times it was more like a rough frontier bar, much akin to the Last Chance saloons of a later day, inevitably attracting all the meaner sort, men whose political "discussions" not infrequently gave over into drunken eye-gouging brawls, one of which was so fierce that Bishop Graff noted despairingly, "Such a thing has never happened here before." And was it Whig or Tory who on one occasion "bit a piece from the under lip" of his opponent?[7]

During the early months of 1777, before the majority of the Tories had been driven into hiding, this sort of thing was almost a daily occurrence. So it is obvious that the Moravians could hardly have stood apart from the events of that day even if that had been their wish, and quite often it was not their wish at all. Traugott Bagge acknowledged more than once that the Brethren were themselves to blame for many of their troubles. The reason, in his view, was that so many of them "were too much and too ignorantly in favor of the old Government, and let this be seen openly."[8]

The opposite was also true, not so much in Salem perhaps as in some of the outlying communities. As Bagge went on to say, it sometimes seemed that everybody in Bethania had "embraced the cause of liberty." Bethania, a divided town from the beginning, having been founded in large part by non-Moravians, was naturally more disposed in favor of independence than the other Wachovia settlements. But none was entirely without its Whig activists—or Tory activists. This division within the Moravian communities was forever manifesting itself in unseemly ways, as when the *Aufseher Collegium* was forced to discipline two Salem youths who had startled the town one evening by exchanging shouts of "Hurrah for King George!" and "Hurrah for Washington!"[9]

Demonstrations of pro-British sentiment occurred less frequently perhaps than those in behalf of independence— again, not because there were so few Tories but because they were a bit more cautious about making their feelings known. Nevertheless, as Bagge said, there were enough such incidents to cause real problems, enough so that the Brethren had to be constantly on guard lest they provide the liberty men with a pretext for raiding their towns and seizing their property. Take the matter of taxes, for instance. As Graff observed, "In some other Districts and Counties the tax matter goes limping or not at all, but we would rather be over particular than give them a chance to get us by the hair, which they would gladly do."[10]

But events had turned against them more rapidly now. One of the first acts of the newly formed North Carolina Assembly was the adoption of a conscription law requiring all able-bodied men between the ages of sixteen and fifty to attend military muster. Justices of the peace, certain other officeholders, ministers, and postmasters were exempt; the Moravians were not. A separate law required all citizens who had kept up their old ties—of whatever sort—with Great Britain to declare their allegiance to the state of North Carolina and at the same time to renounce all fidelity to the king. Not many of the Brethren would have contested the right of the state to swear (or affirm) them to allegiance, but to renounce the king raised far more troublesome questions. Could they do so without compromising the position of their church in England? Would such an affirmation make it impossible for them in good conscience to serve in foreign mission fields still under British dominion?

The answer seemed obvious in both instances. So they held back, and made difficulties. They would appeal, as always to the 1749 Act of Parliament under which they had gained "liberty of conscience," or they might appeal to even more basic rights. Yet all for nothing. The exemptions they had enjoyed under British rule were no longer automatic. In the old days their problems had been mainly political, not legal; now they were both. The 1749 Act could no longer command; it could only suggest, and many of the more radical Whig leaders saw no reason to honor the obligations of a king and Parliament that had done so little to honor their own.

In the fall of 1777 the Moravians took up the matter with their assemblyman Robert Lanier, a Yadkin Valley storekeeper who had just recently uttered "some rather threatening words" against them. This time he was congenial but noncommittal. He vowed "to do his best . . . but thought that the Act would not have much weight under the present Constitution, for as the King had ignored the Charters given to the Colonies so the Colonies had a right to disregard his pledges."[11]

There was some logic and much appeal in this point of view, but no one could have long sustained such an argument on purely philosophical grounds. The question, in other words, was not whether the assemblymen were under some kind of compulsion to obey the dictates of a government they had already repudiated, but whether they would honor the higher imperatives of British law—a system of law that was now the common property of both countries, a system or tradition still wildly imperfect in many ways, and yet remarkably humane by comparison with the spirit of persecution and bloodletting that prevailed throughout most of the world. The people of Britain were still, at that time, far from believing that the punishment of religious error was no business of the state. But the seeds of toleration first planted in those islands and later scattered across the Atlantic had sprung up and yielded a promising crop in the American colonies. Was it not therefore inevitable that the arguments advanced by these Moravians in behalf of religious freedom would eventually prevail? In time, perhaps, but not at the moment. The North Carolina Assembly, angered by Tory uprisings throughout the state and torn by a radical-vs.-conservative split of its own, was in no mood to consider the matter dispassionately. And so the issue remained long in doubt.

Earlier that year, some seven months before the Brethren sought the help of their assemblyman, the sheriff of Surry County had issued a proclamation "ordering all who were in hiding, and all who have shown themselves to be active Tories, to come forthwith and take the Oath of Allegiance to the Commonwealth, or else to remove themselves and their families from the land and go to Lord Howe."[12] At first there was no real effort to force the issue, but as the relatively uneventful year of 1777 turned into a more turbulent and uncertain 1778 the attitude of the Surry Court grew more strident, more menacing. And along with this new show of militance came an even more direct threat: the sudden proliferation of illegal land entries.

So it was no longer a problem of mere legal abstractions or politics. The crucial question now was whether the Brethren would be able to retain ownership of their land, not only the Wachovia tract but also some of the other tracts taken up by

Bishop Spangenberg during his exploratory mission in 1752. Or was it really their land after all? Since none of the Moravian settlers had their names on the deeds there was a widespread assumption that all of their holdings were subject to confiscation under the land tenure acts of 1777. What was often overlooked was that the land had been held in trust for the settlers and was technically no more subject to confiscation than any other piece of American property. The 1782 legislature was finally to confirm the validity of this principle, but there would be no waiting on legal niceties. Many of these wandering bands of frontiersmen simply moved in and settled wherever they chose, fully convinced that the present owners would soon be forced into exile. As Bagge said: "Some went straight to it and entered land in their own names, others hid behind some of the mob and were to share with them in pieces they had entered in their names. So Salem was entered by a lame drummer; Steiner's or Salem mill by an officer; Bethabara and Bethabara mill by a no-account fellow who lived at the home of the Entry Taker; and other good parts of Wachovia were entered by one and another."[13]

The most troublesome of these unauthorized entries occurred in the new county of Wilkes, which had been carved out of Surry in late 1777 and included most of present-day northwest North Carolina. There, some 9,000 acres belonging to the Moravians (or rather held for them in trust) and known as the Mulberry Fields had been designated as the Wilkes courthouse site and for that reason had attracted numerous squatters. "I should have turned them out by force of law," said Bishop Graff, who had taken over supervision of land matters during Frederic Marshall's absence, "but would have been obliged first to take the Oath of Abjuration, so decided to let the land rest and wait for another time."[14] Not long after that Graff managed to sell the Mulberry Fields to a Rowan merchant named Hugh Montgomery, but there still remained the question of who actually owned the land when the transfer took place. Legal technicalities affecting the trusteeship of these tracts, together with political complications arising during and after the war, made it impossible to resolve this question as easily as other aspects of the land controversy. The question was to hang on as a legal issue for more than half a century and was to go before the state Supreme Court seven times before finally being decided in favor of the Unity.

The immediate problem, though, was that the Brethren could find no way to press their land claims without being held up to the laughter and derision of backcountry magistrates and subjected to all sorts of legalistic runarounds. "If a man came to enter land," said Bagge, "he was asked whether he had taken the state oath? If the answer was *Yes* he must be able to prove it twice and thrice; if the answer was *No* he was sent away with mockery and abuse."[15]

There was another way they might have solved the problem. They might have followed the advice of a lawyer who suggested that one of the Brethren take the affirmation and then enter the whole of Wachovia, and presumably the other church-held lands as well, in his own name. The idea must have had some initial appeal. "But when the matter was further considered it was seen that this would only build a bridge to our destruction, so it was not done."[16]

These land controversies plus the newly antagonistic attitude of the Surry Court convinced the Brethren that the time had come to look elsewhere for relief. It was inevitable, of course, that any real relief would have to come from the legislature. Only here might they gain the concessions that no local court was able to grant—or, in failing to gain them, at least come to a better understanding of what might be required to render their fate less onerous.

The problem to which they now addressed themselves really had very little to do with their religious convictions. It was not a question, in other words, of whether their allegiance was to be "sworn" or merely "affirmed"; this was never the central issue at any time during the war, as it had been in other times and in other places. The oath, or affirmation, prescribed by the legislature was unobjectionable except for a single clause: "and I do renounce any Fidelity to the present King of Great Britain, his Heirs & Successors." Strike out that clause and they would gladly profess their allegiance to the new government, though they would still insist on their right not to bear arms.

The truth is that there seems to have been some confusion about what was actually required of them. The affirmation containing this clause had originally been meant only for the

Quakers, but the Moravians assumed, and so apparently did everyone else, that they were subject to the same provisions—not that it would have mattered much one way or the other, since they would have found the oath in its alternate form, that is, in the form prescribed for nonpacifists, even more offensive.

During the early summer of 1778 the Brethren met to plan their strategy and draft their petition for relief. The result of their deliberations was a carefully drawn, persuasive, and even eloquent appeal to the conscience of the state's political leaders, a document in which they again cited the 1749 Act of Parliament even though its validity was no longer recognized, recounted their many battles in behalf of religious freedom, asserted the continuing importance of rights gained under the crown, and implied strongly that, if necessary, they would willingly endure persecution and exile for their beliefs, now as so often in the past. To deliver this petition and somehow convince an uneasy and suspicious assembly that it was no bluff fell to the lot of Traugott Bagge and the Bethabara tavernkeeper, Jacob Blum.

And so the "useful" man Bagge again set out to prove his usefulness to the Moravian cause. By this time he had become the leading man in Wachovia, and was gaining a reputation that would earn him the respect of many non-Moravians, eventually winning him a political following of sorts and getting him elected to the legislature.

But none of this had freed him from the occasional moods of rebelliousness that had darkened his earlier years. Ever the correct diplomat with outsiders, Bagge had found it increasingly difficult to get along with his neighbors and colleagues. On occasion he could be as hot-tempered and intolerant as the potter Aust or his own headstrong assistant, Brother Heckewalder. Christian Reuter, the brilliant surveyor and draftsman largely responsible for the planning of Salem, complained in May of 1775 that Bagge was often against "the order of the community." There was a continuing dispute between the two men over Bagge's plowing of a free street between the community store and Reuter's house, a practice which the surveyor found outrageous and which prevented his coming "to the water."[17]

In that same year Bagge abruptly and without explanation resigned his office as chairman of the *Aufseher Collegium*, leaving behind a residue of profound disgust. "He judges the smallest mistakes of others very harshly and constantly reminds us of trifles in which we are obligated to him,"[18] said a member of the Salem Elders Conference. The Elders esteemed his whole performance so inexcusable that they denied him the right to partake of communion until he had shown some evidence of humility. Throughout these years Bagge's inability to get along with his subordinates—not only Heckewalder, who left Salem in part because of his passionate disagreements with the merchant, but Johann Muschbach, Gottlieb Schober, and others—had been something of a community scandal. But when the times again demanded his participation in the affairs of the *Collegium* the Elders Conference did not hesitate to invite him back as chairman: "In the interest of strengthening the Aufseher Collegium we think it best that Br. Bagge, who laid down his office as chairman, should enter the Collegium again. Certain requisites he demanded as conditions of his coming back have been granted by this conference."[19]

His resumption of that role preceded by only two weeks his crucial visit to Hillsborough, which served briefly as North Carolina's seat of government after the adoption of the 1776 Constitution and the organization of the state legislature. He and Blum left Salem on 4 August, a Tuesday, and breakfasted next morning at Guilford Courthouse, where they learned that the word of their coming was already out and that their petition "was being discussed in a spirit of opposition."[20]

The next day they reached the estate of the worthy Samuel Strudwick, a former king's councilor who had recently taken refuge in Salem in order to avoid swearing allegiance to the new government and who, on his departure, had described the Moravian congregation as "the only practical Christian Society I have ever seen."[21] Strudwick accompanied the two men into Hillsborough, warning them of the legislature's unfriendly mood. Their reception was actually a good bit more hostile than they had been led to expect, for it was now bruited about that the Brethren had been implicated in a recent Tory uprising in Tryon County. "As soon as we alighted, and it was said that we were Moravians, we were told that the ringleaders in Tryon had said under oath that the Moravians knew of their plan and were going to support them."[22]

The rumor pursued them all over Hillsborough. The next afternoon, when they went in and took their seats in the little church where the Commons met, they were immediately forced to defend themselves against the insinuations of "a certain gentleman" in the gallery. Bagge turned on the man and vigorously asserted their innocence. We imagine him in one of his darker moods: grim and even white-faced, perhaps shaking a little, speaking slowly and politely yet with undisguised irritation, the man sitting there silent and Bagge standing looking at him from the floor, inviting him to produce his evidence so that they, the Brethren, might bring the culprit to justice. The performance must have more than satisfied both the man in the gallery and Bagge's many other critics, because from this time on there seems to have been no mention of the Moravians' purported involvement with the Tryon conspirators.

And yet the likelihood that they could win concessions from this body of angry and frustrated men appeared about as hopeless as it had on the day of their arrival. The next morning Bagge accosted Governor Richard Caswell outside the church. The two men spoke and nodded politely—and parted with nothing settled. Caswell made no reference to his earlier doubts about the Moravians, no mention of their "suspicious" visit to Cross Creek in the weeks prior to the Moores Creek encounter. All the same it was quickly apparent that they could expect no real help from him. They called on him that night, at his own suggestion, and found him too busy to talk. Bagge left a copy of the Moravian petition and some other papers for him to read. When he returned the next day to retrieve these papers he felt momentarily encouraged. Caswell adopted an expansive air, assured his visitor that he had nothing but the highest regard for the Moravians, and then hastened to explain that he could do no more than "recommend" them to his friends—that he could not intervene in their behalf "because under the present Constitution he had nothing to say in the Assembly." The leaders of the assembly were less polite and no more helpful. One of them "gave a short and discouraging answer

One of the legislators "gave a short and discouraging answer"
to the Moravian petition, and the other "stole away secretly"

when he was approached on our behalf," and another "stole away secretly" before Bagge had a chance to explain his mission.[23]

It was now Saturday morning, more than a week after their arrival. On the previous day the assembly had set up a joint Senate-House committee to hear the Moravian petition, and now the members of that committee had gathered in a large meeting hall packed with more than a hundred spectators, including the speakers of both houses, to await Bagge's presentation. As he prepared for this task he remembered the text for the day: "Save now, I beseech thee, O Lord; O Lord, I beseech thee, send now prosperity." And for once the omens seemed relatively promising. He had already gained what he regarded as an important tactical advantage by persuading the committee to hear his petition separately from other appeals. He had sought this concession when he learned that a second group of pacifists, the Nicholites, a Quaker splinter group, had come to Hillsborough with a similar petition. He suspected these Nicholites of wanting to combine their cause with that of the Moravians for their own advantage and was anxious to avoid the association at all costs, "as their record was in some respects unsavoury."[24]

The man chosen as chairman of the committee, General Griffith Rutherford, the Rowan militia leader, was something of an unknown quantity. Rutherford had occasionally visited the Wachovia settlements, had complained at least once about the "rights" enjoyed by these Moravians, and had not been particularly scrupulous about respecting those rights since the outbreak of the Revolution. He had frequently given "express orders that the Brethren drill and go into the war"[25]—orders which they had just as frequently ignored. And so even if he did not really believe all that nonsense about the Brethren and the Tryon conspiracy he was apt to be openly hostile to their petition.

As it turned out, his reaction was not exactly what they might have feared. On the whole both he and the other members seemed anxious to provide the Moravians with a fair hearing. Bagge again reviewed the history of their struggles and introduced into the record the original of their Act of Parliament, "which was of more weight than a copy." There was a good response. Two of the members whose attitude was only conjectural now spoke up in a friendly manner, so much so "that the Saviour will surely reward them for it." Even Rutherford seemed to support their appeal. He signed a committee report which lauded the Moravians for their many contributions to the arts and "Manufactures," praised their achievements in agriculture and commerce, paid tribute to their "peaceable & orderly Behaviour," conceded that "they have on all occasions shewed a Readiness to contribute or assist in the common Cause, as far as their religious Scruples of Conscience would admit," and urged the assembly to grant their petition for relief.[26]

But Rutherford obviously had signed the report only because it was expected of him as chairman. Speaking privately with Bagge after the hearing, the general frankly admitted that he did not agree with the committee's findings. At that moment the Moravian spokesman could hardly have failed to remember some of Rutherford's previous complaints about the Brethren— how, for instance, he had once visited the Bethabara tavern and expressed dismay "that the Brethren were the only ones to have a separate Parish, while they, the Presbyterians, had none." In any event there was no real cause for surprise when the general rose on the floor of the Senate and attacked the proposal "with very hard words."[27]

"We sat by, quite comforted and submissive, thinking of the mockery of our Saviour and that His members could not expect better."[28]

Others had even harder words. The Orange County delegate, a Hillsborough lawyer named John Kinchen, took the floor repeatedly, Bagge said, "and painted us in the most horrible colors." Strudwick had warned them about Kinchen. The lawyer apparently felt that he and his entourage had not been treated "with proper consideration" during a 1777 visit to Salem. He accused the Moravians of being contemptuous of the new paper money, which was certainly true to some extent, and of exaggerating their "great Improvements" in Wachovia. He contended, as Bagge went on to say, "that the powerful among us took the property of the weak and sent it no one knew where out of the country; that we were a dangerous Republic within the Republic" and suggested that "if we did not wish to be content with what contented our associate settlers they should send us out of the country and the sooner the better."[29]

The vote was eleven in favor of the petition, thirteen against. After such an outpouring the Brethren might have been surprised that it was even close. Subsequent events helped make it clear, however, that there was more sentiment for the Moravians than had been evident during the formal debate. Three days after the vote, when word came that the Surry court had given them sixty days to take the oath or renounce all claim to their property, even the legislators who had voted against them appeared sympathetic, "for they were all afraid we might leave the country and now each tried to help us." The point is that not all of these men agreed with Kinchen's impassioned speech, even if they happened to agree that the Brethren deserved no special consideration. This may say something about the effectiveness of Bagge's lobbying. But it probably says a lot more about the Moravians' growing reputation as skilled artisans and thrifty farmers, about their ability to supply so many of the scarce articles of war, about the vacant shops and stores that would have been left if they had indeed been forced into exile. Aware of all this, the legislators now rushed to approve a resolution extending until "the sitting of the next General Assembly" the time allowed for the Brethren to take the affirmation, a move that "much displeased" their whiggish neighbors, who really must have begun to believe that they could force the Moravians to throw everything over and flee the country.[30]

In truth, there was never any real chance of that happening, at least not in Bagge's mind. Having done what he could, he now felt that the Brethren might very well take the affirmation in good conscience, and argued in this vein on his return from Hillsborough. He had come to believe that there was no essential difference between the objectionable phrase and the section which would have required them merely to affirm their allegiance to the new state—or rather that the second, more controversial section was fundamentally nothing more than "an amplification of the first part."

"We have had reason to love our former rulers," he said, "and will never hate them, and we have not aided those who have set them to one side, but the King of kings has now placed us under a new Government, and it has the rule over us, and these new rulers demand of us the Affirmation of our fidelity to them, with an Abjuration which follows as a matter of course . . . I do not wish to take the Affirmation, I would rather not take it, I will offer advice to no one, but for myself I have come to think that the taking of the entire Affirmation binds me no further than the taking of the first part would bind me."[31]

The *Collegium* did not agree: "We . . . think that the abjuration is contrary to our conscience, but we will not force Br. Bagge to abide by what we think or do, but will leave him free to take the Oath or not according to his own conscience." Bagge did not sign, but others did, among them his traveling companion Jacob Blum, the Bethabara miller Jacob Kapp, and Philip Transou of Bethania. In the latter community there were widespread expressions of support for the three men, but in his Salem diary Bishop Graff remarked that "true members of the Unity should rather weep over this division."[32]

This does not mean that even he had seriously contemplated the idea of leaving the country. In mulling over that possibility, the bishop concluded that the Brethren probably would not be willing "to give up everything on this account and bring ruin upon their families, especially as no other abiding place can be expected now."[33]

Fortunately the whole question was soon to become academic. When the assembly next convened the Brethren Heckewalder and Gottfried Praetzel were on hand to deliver a second petition for relief. But this time no eloquent speeches were needed. With almost no warning and only perfunctory debate the assembly reversed its previous stand and acceded to every request. Even Kinchen admitted his error and offered his support. The two men left Halifax, where the assembly was then meeting, before the final passage of the act, assured that they and their brethren could now take the oath in a less objectionable form, as in every instance they proceeded to do, and might continue to enjoy their military exemption on condition that they pay a threefold tax. To all of which Graff added a rueful comment: "We were indeed classed with the Quakers, Menonists and Dunkards, but at this time there is nothing else to do."[34]

6

An Audacious Combination

For the first time since the outbreak of the war the Brethren could feel reasonably secure in their legal rights and could even hope for some improvement in their political standing. The same could hardly be said of their economic standing, however. By the spring of 1778 Salem had begun to feel the direct pinch of war and inflation, and had begun to feel it in ways barely imaginable to other less disciplined, less highly organized communities. To help compensate for sharp rises in the cost of living the *Aufseher Collegium* had proposed raising wages of most workers to four shillings a day. But the arrangement did not satisfy everyone. During an April first meeting of the congregation a chronic troublemaker by the name of Ludwig Moeller murmured against the proposal, and later there was "much arguing and complaining" in the Single Brothers' choir house—this also apparently the work of young Moeller, who had ignored an invitation to leave Salem and "seek a wider field" if he didn't like the wage offer.[1]

The next morning there was worse mischief. Town leaders learned upon rising that Moeller and the other young tradesmen had taken to the streets to continue their protest, a protest that would cause them to be remembered as the organizers of North Carolina's first labor strike. First or not, it was an incident calculated to arouse the most intense passions of anger and alarm in this eighteenth-century congregation town. Nothing surely could have struck with more stunning impact at the very foundations of the Moravian social order, an order in which obedience to authority ranked among the supreme virtues—was perhaps the one supreme virtue.

"Their godless intention had been to force a larger increase in their wages," the diarist said, "and to make the officials dance to their piping; the latter, however, were content to leave it to the Saviour to maintain their position against this audacious combination."[2]

They were back from their "pleasure-walk" by nightfall, most of them ready to accept the pay raise as originally proposed and anxious to apologize for "their childish behavior." After they had done ample penance and had had the ways of life in a congregation town explained to them a little more fully, they were accepted back with a "kiss of peace" and with all their old rights restored.

And yet the specter of this new political and economic freedom would not be banished so easily as all that. It is unlikely, of course, that the Brethren had begun to doubt the effectiveness of the strict authoritarian methods by which they had traditionally conducted their affairs. And while they may have foreseen readily enough the extent to which the war and the nonimportation agreement of 1774 would enhance the demand for their products, they may not have foreseen how this rising demand, coupled with the problems of inflation, would gradually undermine the moral and economic discipline that had enabled them to build thriving civilized towns in a place where no towns had ever been.

But they must have already begun to sense what they would not yet quite admit even to themselves. They might first have sensed it when they discovered, some two years before the Single Brothers' abortive walkout, that they could no longer effectively control prices at the retail level—when they discovered, for example, that rapid fluctuations in the cost of cattle and grain had made it impossible for them to calculate the future price of such products as bread and meat. The uncertainties of the wartime market forced them gradually to relinquish their old price-setting function; by 1779 they had relinquished it altogether. When Traugott Bagge sought permission early that year to raise the price of coffee and sugar the *Collegium* sat silent "because it is a matter of the merchants to have the prices lowered and to have them raised."[3]

The real problem was not so much the scarcity of wartime goods, or for that matter the ability of the Moravian tradesmen to keep up with the demand. The real problem was the chaotic condition of the paper currency, made all the worse because no fund had been set up for its redemption. Almost no one trusted the new money, even when he could be sure it wasn't counterfeit. On 9 January 1778 Bishop Graff reported that "confusion increases among the people" and "all are intent on getting rid of their new money; in Bethabara a man sold a barrel of tar for 10 shillings silver rather than take 48 shillings Congress money, and so it goes with everything. Br. Bagge thinks he will entirely stop the sale of certain articles."[4]

Yet hard money was scarce, had always been scarce, and obviously was to become scarcer still. Since the British had never permitted the minting of gold and silver in the colonies and since the balance of trade lay always with the mother country, there was never enough specie to meet the ordinary demands of trade, much less the extraordinary demands of war. Colonial assemblies had periodically issued bills of credit to make up the lack and some merchants also accepted tobacco warehouse receipts, personal promissory notes, and other forms of paper as legal tender. North Carolina had floated its first issue of paper in 1712 during a war with the Tuscaroras.

But all of this was in a time when government wore a cloak of stability—and respectability. The Declaration of Independence had gained the Americans much respect for the rights of man but little in the way of a stable government, and there had seldom been less reason for public confidence than in this winter of 1778–1779. Hard-working tradespeople and farmers now looked about with new disappointment and with a sense of growing uncertainty. Until the closing stages of the war many of these people, particularly those in the Moravian settlements, where loyalist sentiment was seldom very far below the surface, doubted very much that the colonies would ever achieve the freedom they had proclaimed so loudly in the summer of 1776. As a result the paper currency, whether in the form of Continental dollars or North Carolina Congress money, was little more than a joke and was understood as such by Tory and Whig alike. Hard money of almost any description— Spanish pistole, French guinea, English halfpence—was infinitely preferable. And it was to no avail that the government passed rigorous laws to prevent the depreciation of its bills of exchange, since no one ever found a way to enforce these edicts. The money was worth whatever it would purchase in a given vicinity at a given time, and that varied almost from week to week, and, indeed, in the years after 1779, almost from day to day.

For some of the Moravian tradesmen—men like the potter Aust and the tanner Peter Yarrell—the money was unacceptable even at the most exaggerated rate of exchange. To avoid getting stuck with it Yarrell sometimes swapped finished leather goods for such things as nails, indigo, coffee, and spices, and either swapped or sold these commodities in competition with the Salem store. Traugott Bagge warned that Yarrell's "deals" would inevitably lead to a breakdown in community financial regulations, and the *Collegium* promptly agreed that no wares sold in the store should be "sold in some other place."5 The store, like the pottery, the red tannery, and the tavern, was still a church-owned enterprise, and all profits from retail sales were to be placed at the disposal of the church *Diaconie*.

There is little evidence that the *Collegium*'s frequently stern admonitions had much effect on Yarrell. And it is certain that they had none on Aust, whose crime was all the greater in that he not only made profitable deals on the side but roundly scorned the paper currency in front of anybody who would listen, presumably including some of the same politicians who had authorized the soft-money plan and whose friendship was essential if the Moravians' claim to military exemption was to be upheld. The *Collegium* "noted with lament" Brother Aust's many offenses and warned the potter that his unguarded comments were sure to bring "loss and harm to the whole community." But Aust went on talking as he had always talked and trading as he had always traded. Like Yarrell, he would accept silver when he could get it and bartered goods when he could not. At one point he had accumulated such a store of commodities—tallow, cotton, flax—that the *Collegium* ordered the whole inventory placed in Bagge's keeping. Another time the *Collegium* simply confiscated his money, not "because we did not have any money, but because we did not want him to have all the money lying around"; and then chided him for wanting his share of the pottery income doled back in a value larger than "he has given it."[6]

None of this is to suggest that these two men were the only offenders. Once, when Brother Johann Heinzmann, the Single Brothers' *vorsteher*, refused to accept ten pounds of Congress money in payment of a debt, Brother Christian Triebel threatened to seek relief from the civil authorities. Bagge himself would take the money only with great reluctance, preferring when at all possible to give out his wares on credit "till we have better times." Even the upright *Collegium*, for all of its complaints about Yarrell and Aust, was never anxious to accept the money in payment of town bills. But members usually succeeded in overcoming their own better judgment, reminding themselves as well as the townspeople not to refer to the currency as "rebel money" or as "the money of some scoundrels."[7]

In the spring of 1779 the *Collegium* noted: "We do not mean to repudiate the paper money, we have no right to do that and do not wish it, and we will be obliged to continue to accept it in trade, especially at the tavern, from officers, from our present government officials, and from soldiers on the march."[8]

And again, after the war was already over: "Several people have uttered very hostile expressions against Salem and have threatened us, because of the paper money. For that reason we think that it will be best that the branches where the money comes in do not refuse it any more."[9]

And so the men of the community watched with mounting dismay as the money, both legal and counterfeit, piled up in their shops and stores. Even Aust and Yarrell were forced to take it in occasionally. The excellence of the Moravian wares, their good brandy and wholesome beer, their now not altogether enviable reputation as the leading trade center of the whole backcountry—all of these things together with the heavy influx of military traffic had conspired to bring down on them this vast store of unwanted wealth, the more so since customers usually preferred to take their change in goods rather than in paper. As Bagge described the process: "If there was some part due on a bill they wanted to spend they would say, if in the tavern: 'Give me a dram for it'; in the store: 'Give me some thread, needles, tape, sugar,' or whatever; to the tanner it was: 'Give me a strap, a pair of soles'; to the potter: 'Give me another pipe,' etc. So the time began when it was a real problem to spend the money that one was obliged to take in."[10]

The problem occupied increasing amounts of their time. Quite often after a brisk interval of trade Brother Christian Heckewalder or Brother George Bibighaus would hitch up the wagon teams and go racing south to Cross Creek or Charleston where, God willing, they would be able to swap the money for "indigo, negroes or something else that has real worth to it."[11] But they were never able to get rid of it at anything like the rate at which they had taken it in. They would trade, say, on a basis of 4 paper dollars to 1 hard dollar and then find that the rate had jumped to 5½ to 1 or maybe even 8 to 1 before they had a chance to get rid of it. The teamsters thought they had done well when on one occasion they exchanged about five thousand pounds in paper money for goods valued at no more than 12 percent of that amount: a Negro boy, some shoe leather and joiner's tools, a worm for their distillery, a set of weights and measures, and an assortment of iron and other goods for the Salem store. When Brother Samuel Stotz returned to Cross Creek a year later, he was forced to trade on a basis of 125 paper dollars to 1 dollar of specie. This was the Continental currency of which George Washington had said, "Our money does but pass." But the North Carolina bills of credit were even more worthless, Stotz being forced to trade these off on a basis of about 200 to 1. Before the end of the war the disparity had grown so great—about 800 to 1—that any hope of actually achieving a stable rate of exchange was now wholly out of the question.

It had never really been possible anyway, and the Moravian leaders had understood that almost from the beginning—had understood the need for stern anti-inflationary measures even before the disastrous budget year of 1780, when the congregation *Diaconie* reported losses totaling more than one thousand pounds. At one point they had devised an ingenious plan whereby they would accept as little paper money as possible from outsiders and circulate none at all among themselves. Instead, they would estimate the worth of everything on its old hard-money basis and circulate a kind of scrip based on that value. This scrip would pass current for all of their own needs, and could be exchanged for real money when the economy gained stability. "But the plan would not go."[12]

Opponents assailed the proposal as unworkable and laid the whole thing to politics. Their attitude provoked a somewhat bitter response from Bishop Graff: "We officials have done what our duty imposed upon us, but as our plan is not accepted, and has been made the occasion of giving utterance to private grudges and mistrust, though no valid objection has been offered, we will drop the matter until the Brethren themselves see the necessity of such an arrangement, or some other which would serve the same purpose."[13]

Eventually the Brethren did adopt a modified form of this plan, trading among themselves on a strict hard-money basis and as best they could with outsiders. Of the inflated currency they were obliged to take in, they used as much of it as possible to pay their taxes. (There is no evidence that state authorities were any more anxious to have it back than they were to pay it out.) They also relied heavily on credit and on a kind of barter system to get them through the last years of the war. But the question at the moment was whether any of this would be enough. "May God soon give us better times," the bishop lamented, "or our finances will come into the greatest distress."[14] The cry was a universal one.

7
October Days

The country rings around with loud alarms,
And raw in fields the rude militia swarms:
Mouths without hands, maintained at vast expense,
In peace a charge, in war a weak defense,
Stout once a month they march, a blustering band,
And ever, but in time of need, at hand.
This was the morn when, issuing on the guard,
Drawn up in rank and file, they stood prepared
Of seeming arms to make a short essay,
Then hasten to be drunk, the business of the day.
John Dryden, Cymen and Iphigenia

Such were the ordeals of muster day in the Britain of
Charles II, a hundred years or more before the outbreak of the
American Revolution, a hundred years during which England
had advanced from the rank of a secondary power dependent
for defense on a raw unformed body of soldiery to one of
unparalleled military supremacy. But Dryden's lines express
equally well how the American colonists of a later day, the
Moravians not least of all, felt about their own poorly armed,
poorly trained, undisciplined, and ill-led militiamen, who
bullied civilians, fled from battle, and seemed ever at hand "but
in time of need."

A passage describing what had come to be a typical
experience for many of the Moravian settlers appears in the

Friedberg diary for December of 1778: "At noon we were suddenly startled, for someone let us know that soldiers were coming to plunder as they had already done at Ebert's. We had scarcely time to put a few things out of sight when they appeared. The Press-Master came into the school-room with an air of great authority, but saw there was nothing they wanted; then they looked in the chimney for what might be hidden there, found a crupper and took it."[1]

Often there were more serious alarms. On the previous day the same diarist, the Friedberg minister John Valentine Beck, had reported: "Quite early the elder Spach came to us in much distress. He said that the preceding night a Captain had come from camp and had entered his house to take his son, and when he did not find him he threatened that if the son was not delivered to him in two days, or a man provided to take his place, he would ruin Spach. The latter was ready to try to find a man, and I could neither advise him for or against, for he had already tried in vain to have him released for a fine, and to be ruined would be very hard."[2]

With the passage of the 1779 law exempting Moravians from military service Spach and his son would have less reason to fear such threats. Nevertheless, he and the other villagers would experience far more terrible days before the end of the war. No town lay more open to assault than Friedberg. Lying as it did mostly in Rowan County and therefore beyond the protection of the friendly Surry commander, Colonel Martin Armstrong, the Friedberg settlement was often a focal point of terror, its citizens being robbed, cursed, beaten, stomped on, and shot at even more frequently perhaps than residents of the larger Moravian communities to the north. From the front of his new stone house Adam Spach could stand and look out across three hundred yards of rolling, thinly wooded landscape and see the troops moving along the main north-south road between Salem and Salisbury. And as he stood there he might have prayed that this time at least they would not turn west to assault his family or requisition his livestock, or perhaps drag his son off to a war that must have seemed to both of them wasteful, sad, and, most of all, incomprehensible.

Spach, a native of Alsace, had long admired the Herrnhut teachings before settling in Carolina and joining the Moravian

Church. He had been attending worship services in Bethabara when his only neighbors in the future village of Friedberg were the wolves and bears and panthers, and when Bethabara itself was only a rude settlement recently hacked out of the wilderness. Probably there was no man in all of Wachovia more respected than Adam Spach, no man more devout, no man more exemplary of the ancient Moravian virtues, a pacifist in the mold of Peter of Chelcicky and other early church leaders, a man of great physical strength and supremely valiant, and yet a man who would fight for nothing so tenaciously as his right to remain a disciple of peace, a quiet man, in the face of the direst threat and most fatal alarm, who fought now for his son as he had once fought for himself.

"I will not attend muster, and will bear whatever that may bring upon me," he had told the Reverend Ludolph Bachhof shortly before the latter's death. "I wish that they all thought as I do, then one day in each week we would meet in the School-House, and unitedly lay the difficult circumstances upon the heart of the Saviour, instead of going to Muster once a month."[3]

Meantime the war had been going badly for the American forces. There had been fighting in Georgia, in the pine flats south of Charleston, in Charleston itself, and along the border between North and South Carolina, the Continentals steadily giving ground before the disciplined legions of Lord Charles Cornwallis and Banastre Tarleton. And now, more than ever, great numbers of hastily assembled militiamen swarmed along the high road between Bethabara and Salem and between Salem and Friedberg, leaving behind a trail of mayhem, of robbed homes and empty granaries and, in the summer of 1779, a smallpox epidemic that took four lives.

It was a summer different from all other summers, a summer of echoes, of ghostly footsteps, and desolate voices. There was almost no one on the streets. Except for "an occasional emaciated Militia-man,"[4] the townspeople saw little to remind them of the war. The few civilians who had to come to town on business often stuck tobacco leaves in their nostrils, or smeared tar on their foreheads or over their lips, or found other nostrums which they hoped would ward off the disease.

The epidemic hung on till October. Inoculation, then the most advanced means for coping with smallpox, and the only means for cutting short the life of an epidemic, was not unknown in Salem; and the Brethren would have gone ahead and introduced the disease in this manner except for the rantings of a Richmonder named John Snead, who "threatened to destroy the town if we inoculated." Snead's reaction was perhaps more violent but otherwise no different from the reaction of most Americans. The idea of inoculating healthy individuals with smallpox in order to produce a milder form of the disease and to produce it at a time of year when the body was best able to withstand the onslaught had made only limited headway even in the sophisticated metropolitan centers of Europe, and almost none at all in America. In this country the mere mention of inoculation was enough to bring a storm of rocks and threatening messages crashing through a do-gooder's window. And so the Brethren waited it out, once again held in thrall by their "ignorant and malicious neighbors."[5]

Even at that, the epidemic seems to have been as welcome in some ways as the numerous detachments of "rude militia" that had once descended on the town. Bishop Graff's diary entry for 23 June is indicative: "Few children are left who can be counted well, and they are very anxious to have small-pox, and visit the sick gladly." A few days later he reported that Traugott Bagge's nine-year-old daughter Elisabeth, "who has often wept because she was the only little girl who did not have small-pox, has now taken it."[6]

These were also the years of the great migration to the new land beyond the Cumberlands, the land of "Kentuk," the migrants driving their herds of cattle through the dusty Moravian towns and giving Bishop Graff cause to wonder how "such a crowd of people as are going thither will be able to support themselves." He might have wondered too whether they would find anything other than what they had sought to escape—more wars, more Indian troubles. Some weeks earlier, Daniel Boone had stopped in Salem to report that he had been "recently seized by the English near the Salt Springs in Kentuk, but escaped." Other visitors brought similar news. One of them, the "well-known old Nef," an eighty-year-old veteran of the Continental wars, reported "that the Indians are still murdering in that neighborhood, and the people are retiring into the forts."[7]

But mainly now the war came up from the south. With the approach of the British, the Tories along the Yadkin rose with a shout and a great mustering of arms. After the rout of American forces at Stono Ferry and Charleston, Samuel Bryan, son of the Indian trader Morgan Bryan, raised a company of some eight hundred men and moved south by forced marches to join the British. And then, in a series of engagements along the Carolina border, Bryan was himself routed, because now the Whigs had risen too. Throughout the spring and early summer of 1780 these volunteer units, fighting under such patriot leaders as Griffith Rutherford and William R. Davie and greatly encouraged by the slowness of Lord Cornwallis's northward advance, harried the British troops and their Tory allies almost without letup, winning significant "partisan" victories at Ramsour's Mill, at Hanging Rock, South Carolina, and at Colson's Mill on the Pee Dee, where Bryan fought. So vehement was Lord Cornwallis's reception that his second in command, the insufferable Banastre Tarleton, declared the counties of Rowan and Mecklenburg to be "more hostile to England than any others in America."[8] But though the Whigs often seemed to get the best of it in secondary battles, the British consistently won the major engagements. The fall of Camden, South Carolina, where there was some of the fiercest fighting of the war, again dashed American hopes; and by fall Cornwallis was in Charlotte.

And now as September came on, bringing rain to alleviate the long drought, Wachovia itself seemed on the verge of open warfare. There would be brief intervals of brooding calm, and then all at once the soldiers would appear, anonymous, brutal, smelling of drink and the smoke of battle, regulars and deserters alike, some of them fleeing a war they did not yet quite understand, others shamed perhaps into returning to an action they had too hastily fled, men of every possible faith and allegiance, some kindly enough, but all too many of them drunken and violent, prowling about the dusty Salem streets, assaulting the tradesmen and shopkeepers, disrupting worship services, driving their horses through the oats and corn, commandeering grain and beef, ball and shot, leather goods, cattle, horses and wagons, and whipping Tories in the public squares.

The Tory hunt had begun in late August, under the capable leadership of Colonel William Campbell of the Virginia militia. Campbell and his 300-man army, joined by a much smaller detachment under Martin Armstrong, spent almost three weeks scouring Wachovia and the surrounding countryside for fugitive loyalists. The captives were brought hogtied and unpenitent into Bethabara, the principal rendezvous point for the roundup. "There things went badly because of the numbers present," Frederic William Marshall later recalled, "and Bethabara suffered in many ways—in her corn-fields, meadows, and orchards, at the mill, in the brewery and distillery, where all the reserve stores were taken."9

On the morning of 8 September the Brethren learned that a Guilford County highwayman and Tory captain named Nathan Read "was to be hanged, and that here in our town." The doomed man was already on the square and the soldiers drawn up in good order when some of the Brethren sought the intervention of Colonel Armstrong. Armstrong's only concession was to shift the execution away from the center of town. By the time the Tory-hunters were ready to string their man up, the Brethren had become a bit more reconciled, and so apparently had the man on the gallows, for he now readily admitted "that he deserved his sentence and ought to die quickly."10

And so it went almost everywhere, even in such out-of-the-way places as Hope, the "English Settlement" founded earlier that year on the eastern slopes of Muddy Creek and served by the Moravian minister, John Christian Fritz. It was there on a hot night in mid-September that a crowd of liberty men led by a certain Captain Holston crashed into a room where Brother Fritz and his wife lay sleeping. The men lurched about wildly, drunkenly, brandishing their swords. Ordered out of bed and forced to open their clothing chests, Brother and Sister Fritz watched helplessly as their visitors cleaned out everything: dresses, jackets, socks, gowns, linen, even the shirt Brother Fritz was wearing, whereupon the minister at last "found courage to speak seriously with the Captain, asking him whether he and his men robbed and plundered like Tories."[11] Brother Fritz spoke in such lugubrious yet imperative tones that the captain fell into a horrible fit of remorse and urged him to worry no longer about the stolen articles: he would see to it that they were all brought back before a single man slept. And so they were, all except a piece of linen which he was unable to retrieve until later that evening, and which was returned early the next day as he and his men were preparing to flee across the Yadkin ahead of a gang of pursuing Tories.

An unusual tribute, perhaps, to Brother Fritz's powers of persuasion.

But what was Brother Jacob Pfeil to say when, under similar circumstances, he watched a group of soldiers snatch the silver shoe buckles off his feet?

Or Brother Jeremias Schaaf when told that his clothing had been stolen out of his washtub?

Or Sister Marie Baumgarten when she learned that all of the butter had been stolen out of her milkhouse and the crock left broken in a yard near Salem Square?

Or Brother Joseph Booner who was stopped on the street and casually "beaten half to death"?[12]

Or brother Martin Schneider when he started to pour himself a glass of his wild grape wine only to discover that the soldiers had already drunk it all and refilled the keg with water?

By the time the last of these liberty men had finished their work there was barely enough left of the bountiful Moravian harvest to sustain the next group of marauders, the next gang of Tory-hunters. Even before the worst of the siege the stockpiles of food and other goods had dropped alarmingly. In early September when Colonel Armstrong and Colonel Campbell had begun looking for a supply of grain they "found that not as much can be secured in this district as Captain Paschke had led them to expect."[13] As with all people in all wars, it was now a common practice for the Brethren to tie up their horses and cattle in the woods and to store their grain in places not so conspicuous to passing soldiers. And in Salem Brother Jacob Meyer, the tavernkeeper, was soon to take the unusual step of removing his street sign (after receiving from the *Aufseher Collegium* grudging permission to do so) as a way of discouraging unwanted military traffic. But still the soldiers came, sometimes singly or in small partisan bands, or sometimes in whole companies, appearing suddenly and without warning in the streets of Salem or on the low-lying meadows below Bethabara, often with prisoners in tow, often alone, and always full of bluster and the gravest of threats.

But none of this left the Brethren completely without recourse. When one of these militiamen became convinced that Salem was not responding quickly enough to his request for medical assistance and promised to return with 150 companions and set fire to the town, Bishop Graff muttered that "he will not be able to do this unless our Lord gives His consent."[14]

Through all of this the Moravian leaders fervently guarded their still somewhat tentative rights of neutrality, refusing to grant certificates of exemption to communicants who had not paid the required threefold tax and admonishing even the most faithful to beware of expressions of support for the British government. There had never been a time when the temptation to throw in with the loyalists was more appealing. This was after the American calamity at Camden and before the totally unexpected victory at Kings Mountain, and thus a time when the Continental forces seemed mired in the mud of permanent defeat. "The people are in the extreme of fright because of the English,"[15] the bishop declared, so much so that some of them had been misled into a "premature declaration" in favor of the loyalist cause.

Graff was speaking primarily of non-Moravians, but there was good reason to fear that many of the Brethren, the less cautious ones, would eventually yield to similar pressures. Worse, there was a widespread impression outside Wachovia that most of them already had. In early June a refugee from Georgia, Colonel Joseph Haversham, had appeared in Salem with his Negroes and cattle and expressed surprise at his cordial reception, "for he had heard that we were Tories, and had not expected such courtesy." This was an impression the Moravian leaders were never able to dispel completely, even though they began to speak out ever more harshly against Tory sympathizers. Typical was a reminder that the Brethren were "not to permit the hated name 'Tory' to be applied to them, for they have proved the contrary by taking the Affirmation and paying the threefold tax."[16]

And yet despite these warnings, despite their indulgence of unruly soldiers and pressmasters, despite repeated attempts to clarify their position, despite Bishop Graff's now-habitual reference to the new American government as "our" government, despite all of this it became increasingly difficult with each new British victory to convince the rough backcountry folk, who often wanted an excuse to plunder anyway, that these Moravian Brethren, so peaceful in outward appearance, yet with their strange language and stranger ways, were not in fact dedicated Tories, secretly storing ammunition, grain, and other supplies against the arrival of the British troops, at which time they would rise up like all the forces of the Antichrist and reveal the full measure of their guile by openly casting their lot with Lord Cornwallis.

Of the many backcountry settlers who had already sided with the British we really know very little. Among them were the men who had ridden with Bryan and others who would ride with Colonel Gideon Wright. It may be that many of them chose this course not so much out of loyalty to the king as out of respect for their neighborhood leaders. Bryan is said to have gained most of his support in this manner, and also to have lost some in the same way. Legend has it that some of the members of his company made their choice on the basis of a previously arranged fistfight between the colonel (then captain) and one of his lieutenants, Richmond Pearson, who had swung over to the side of independence. Pearson came from a section known as the Forks of the Yadkin and evidently had won the support of most of the young men in that neighborhood. On the appointed day he and Bryan slugged it out, with Pearson the clear winner, and from that time on, or so the story goes, "the Fork company was for liberty, and Bryan's crowd, on Dutchman's Creek, were loyalists."[17]

As active as the Tories were, they never quite gained the ascendancy, either politically or militarily, and so were often driven from their homes and forced to band together into robber gangs. One of the most notorious of the loyalist strongholds was in present-day Stokes County, just north of the Sauratown mountains, in a cave long known as the "Tory House." The bones of many a lawless feast lay piled high in the door of this "house," and for many years after the war there were tales about the monstrous behavior of the occupants—how, for instance, they had once "killed five head of horses belonging to Matthew More, a prominent Whig in that region, by knocking them in the head with their tomahawks."[18]

Some of these "outlyers," these occupants of the Tory House and others like them, had been driven from their farms quite early in the war, and now others were driven out to join them, not only the men this time but the women too. In August of 1780 the Bethania diarist reported: "Several women passed. Their husbands joined those in favor of the king, and now the women have been driven from their farms and told to go to their husbands. They were helped to food and drink, so that they could continue their journey."[19]

Were the Moravians next? In late August Bishop Graff heard that a company of light horse had "beaten several men" and had threatened the Salem miller Jacob Steiner with similar treatment, "claiming that he had spoken against *Liberty*."[20] By early fall conditions had grown so ominous that the Congregation Council was moved to adopt what was perhaps its most striking declaration of neutrality and pacifism of the entire war:

It is our duty, in speaking with outsiders about our position in these political circumstances, that we allow no one to doubt that we are faithful subjects to the State. Even without an Affirmation our conscience would have required that we be loyal to the State, according to Romans 13: 1–7, but in addition we have taken the Affirmation in the sight of God. Our character as an honorable people requires that we maintain this position, so that every one may acknowledge us as faithful subjects of the State, which will give us standing with this party, and will not bring us into danger from their opposers, for in all the world it is required that fidelity be pledged to the party of government that is in power, and that due submission shall be made to it. It is painful for us, it is unendurable, and in the end dangerous, if we permit ourselves to be accused of being Tories, and we are to consider this term of reproach as an injury, not as dishonor to be borne for the sake of Christ, and we shall not let it rest upon us.[21]

And then in late October came news of the startling American victory at Kings Mountain. In that battle a company of rangy mountain men, angered by Colonel Patrick Ferguson's threat to hang their leaders and lay waste their farms and villages, stormed a seemingly unassailable redoubt and, with longrifles blazing, shot the enemy into submission and themselves into instant legend. But Kings Mountain was only the most spectacular of a whole series of battles fought between self-recruited bands of irregulars during those last months before Cornwallis's invasion of North Carolina. Actually there were British regulars as well as Tories at Kings Mountain; in essence, however, it was the same kind of battle that Ramsour's Mill had been, or Hanging Rock, or Colson's Mill—all of them battles fought primarily between neighbors and, in some cases, the closest of kin. These were the battles that have led historians to characterize the fighting in the Carolinas as civil war in its purest form, a war that raged apart from, and yet as a part of, the larger war of the Revolution.

Earlier in the month this partisan war had broken out like a rash all over the upper Piedmont, culminating in a series of sharp engagements between first one and then another group of Whigs and the followers of Colonel Gideon Wright, whose younger brother had been subjected to a whiplashing during the recent Tory hunt at Bethabara. The first word of Wright's activities had come on 8 October, when he and his men conducted a hit-and-run raid on Richmond town. Four days later, on a rainy Thursday, prior to what has become known as the "First Battle of the Shallow Ford," the Tory army appeared in Bethania to inquire after the whereabouts of liberty men. "It can be considered a direct act of Providence that the last of the Liberty Men set out scarcely an hour earlier," said the local diarist, "for the town has been full of them since Monday."[22] There were perhaps a hundred men with Wright that morning, all of them remaining astride their horses while the people of Bethania served them breakfast.

Later that day Wright and his men clashed with a company of Whigs out of Bethabara. Someone yelled for the Whigs to surrender; they refused. There was a burst of musket fire and then a brief hand-to-hand skirmish in which one and possibly two patriots were killed and the others put to flight. The news of this success must have brought the Tories flocking to Wright's standard. It would seem so, at any rate, judging by the

The colonel and his loyalist followers remained astride their horses while the men of Bethania served them breakfast

accounts which reached Salem late that afternoon and the next day. In his Salem diary Bishop Graff reported that the Tory army had marched some five hundred strong past the Bethabara mill, "but without molesting anything."

"It looks now as though the entire Tory party had risen," he wrote, "both in this neighborhood and on Abbots Creek."[23]

This was on Friday. All that day random bands of these king's men were still moving through the Moravian settlements. In Bethania there was a second visit from a hundred or so Tories who had come through about midnight and had gone off in a fruitless search for Colonel Wright. It was still quite early when they reappeared in the Bethania streets. Close behind them came sixteen other members of the party: wild, angry, arm-waving horsemen who gave it out that they had been shot at on their way into the village. The townspeople assured them that no one in Bethania would have fired the shots and that it was "probably the act of spies, whom they had not seen."[24] The horsemen seem to have believed this unlikely story, for they confiscated only a horse and a musket while they were in town and left with no further attempts to alarm the villagers.

And maybe it was the act of spies after all. The town minister and diarist, John Jacob Ernst, must have thought so. The next day, Saturday, he reported that all was quiet "except that in town and in the woods several were seen who might have been spies."[25]

By Saturday morning Wright had reached the Shallow Ford. Here the Yadkin spreads itself thin between wide banks. In some places the bottomlands stretch away unbroken toward the distant rim of the Blue Ridge mountains; at others the slopes rise almost sheer from the water's edge. It was probably no later than ten o'clock when the colonel and his now-sizable Tory army came down out of the cup of hills that guards the eastern approach to the river. About them a shimmer of October flame: the pale russets and golds and mottled scarlets of the gum and oak forests now brilliantly alive in spite of the rain and heavy mist. Wright may have had as many as nine hundred men with him that morning; a better guess is that he had no more than half that number. Once across the river, they would move quickly down the west bank to join Cornwallis in Charlotte. The colonel had already sent some of his men ahead "to get a way open for them to join the British army.''[26] This was the same route Cornwallis himself was to travel some four months hence when he came north in pursuit of a rapidly retreating American army under General Nathanael Greene.

But Wright's hopes for glory in the loyalist cause were destined to end right there in the sand and mud flats of the Shallow Ford; because now the alarm was out, and somewhere between the high ground and the water the patriot forces came swooping down on him with a glint of steel and a withering burst of musket and rifle fire. Within moments a dozen or more Tories lay dead, four others were seriously wounded, and the rest had vanished, seemingly forever, into the raindamp woods and swamps or back along the road whence they had come. Major Joseph Cloyd and a force of some one hundred and sixty Virginia and North Carolina militiamen had carried the main assault. A detachment of some three hundred foot soldiers commanded by Colonel John Paisley came up in time to witness the scene and may have joined in the late fighting. Yet another force, this one a 150-man detachment under General William Smallwood, arrived much too late for the battle and spent most of the next day in Salem, the soldiers "cooking in the open place by the Tavern in the heavy rain."[27]

Out of these few facts have come many legends. An oral tradition prevalent in Yadkin and Davie counties insists that this battle was actually fought on the opposite side of the river, after Wright and his men had already started their long march south. But this is only a tradition, borne out by none of the written accounts. The Moravian Records suggest that the battle occurred on the east bank, and General Smallwood's report seems to confirm this. The way he described it was that Wright and his men "had *attempted* to cross the Shallow Ford, but were attacked and defeated by Major Cloyd."[28] Nevertheless, the tradition is so enduring and so fraught with plausible detail that we would be foolish to dismiss it entirely. The truth is that there may have been some fighting, perhaps even intense fighting, on both sides of the river. It was on the west bank, for example, that a Captain Francis of Wilkes County, the only Whig fatality, is said to have lost his life. There are stories too about the furious fighting along Battle Creek just west of Huntsville, about how Captain Joseph Williams, who lived just east of the

Yadkin, had "come over for the fight" and had stomped on a wounded Tory named Skidmore, how Skidmore got up in spite of his wounds and fled to safety, and how the patriots clubbed and shot at the wounded Tories as they attempted to get back across the river.[29]

Oral tradition further insists that none of this really happened in October at all—that all of these stories, these legends, are associated with Cornwallis's crossing four months later. Even the name Battle Creek is associated with a later skirmish presumed to have taken place on the west bank of the river and sometimes described as the "Second Battle of the Shallow Ford." But there seems to have been no such battle. The most venerable of North Carolina's Revolutionary authorities, the nineteenth-century minister and author Eli W. Caruthers, does not mention it. Nor do the Moravian Records. Nor is there any word of it in the writings of Cornwallis or his fellow officers. The only engagement that could remotely qualify as a second Battle of the Shallow Ford occurred some time after Cornwallis was across the river and marching for Bethania, and even this was nothing more than an inconsequential skirmish between an American cavalry unit and some few British soldiers who had hung too far back out of the line of march. It thus seems indisputable that the Battle Creek legends are merely the remembered fragments of the earlier engagement fought in October of 1780. In any case the Battle of the Shallow Ford, the first one, finally brought to an end all organized Tory resistance in this part of the Piedmont, and we hear no more of Colonel Gideon Wright until his death late in 1782.

A week or so after the battle some two hundred and fifty prisoners taken at Kings Mountain, accompanied by perhaps twice that many guards, appeared in Bethabara. They would spend more than two weeks in the town, the British officers lodged in private homes and the common soldiers in an abandoned store. For their Tory allies a worse punishment was waiting: these men, who made up the bulk of the prisoners, were herded into a small cattle pen outside of town and left there with no protection against the rain and cold and with nothing to eat except "raw meat and raw corn from the cob."[30] The liberty men hoped by this means to force the prisoners to renounce the king and join the common cause. This was a favorite device during the Revolution and one that had seldom worked as effectively as in the present instance. Before the end of their eighteen-day captivity all but a very few of the prisoners had chosen to enlist in the American armies, with some additional encouragement perhaps from the Baptist preacher William Hill.

On the first Sunday after their arrival in Bethabara, a day unexpectedly bright and warm, Hill was on hand to commemorate the victories at Kings Mountain and Shallow Ford, preaching "earnestly on the 63rd chapter of Isaiah."[31] One can imagine the scene: the prisoners and their heavily armed guards and more than fifteen hundred of the country folk gathered in the big meadow below the Bethabara mill, the grass still damp from the recent showers and the people standing not only in the meadow but in the surrounding woods. And there, in front of them, the Reverend Mr. Hill striding rapidly back and forth along a high treeless embankment, sweating in the moist October air, shouting, arms waving, preaching again of vengeance and heavenly wrath and also of loving kindness and the great goodness of God, a message in every way typical of the New Light sermons heard so frequently in those days:

I have trodden the winepress alone; and of the people there was none with me; for I will tread them in mine anger, and trample them in my fury; and their blood shall be sprinkled upon my garments, and I will stain all my raiment.

For the day of vengeance is in mine heart, and the year of my redeemed is come.

And I looked, and there was none to help; and I wondered that there was none to behold: therefore mine own arm brought salvation unto me; and my fury, it upheld me.

And I will tread down the people in mine anger, and make them drunk in my fury, and I will bring down their strength to the earth.

8

No More Rivers to Cross

Now we have come to what in some ways is the most memorable period of the entire war. In spite of the victory at Kings Mountain, which had forced Cornwallis to abandon Charlotte and take up winter quarters in Winnsboro, South Carolina, the year 1780 had ended with the American armies near total collapse. Then a new general, Nathanael Greene, appeared in the American ranks, and a new war took shape. A brilliant strategist and meticulous planner, Greene immediately committed what many of his advisers felt was a fatal error: he divided his army in the face of an opposing force much larger than his own. While the main body retired to Cheraw, South Carolina, a ragged and half-starved detachment of regulars and indifferently armed militiamen, under the command of Brigadier General Daniel Morgan, marched rapidly south with orders to put themselves between the British and the mountains. Cornwallis countered by dividing his own army. The job of stopping Morgan fell to the capable and often vicious Banastre Tarleton, whose 550-man Legion, an elite corps of dragoons and light infantrymen, was reinforced by some two hundred of Cornwallis's most dependable regulars.

On the morning of 17 January the two generals faced each other at a place called Hannah's Cowpens, a rolling, sparsely wooded stretch of grazing land in the South Carolina foothills. Drawn up amid a thin cover of trees, with a swollen river at their back, the Americans awaited a battle in which victory was unlikely and flight impossible. They had crouched there since first dawn, with an icy mist in their faces, blowing on their trigger fingers to keep them warm, a force of men vastly inferior to the British in numbers, arms, training, and in almost every other way, yet faced with the certain knowledge that a loss in this remote part of the world would enable Cornwallis easily to knock off the rest of the American army and bring both of the Carolinas under British domination.

But then something happened which even today cannot be adequately explained.

Generations of school children have read about the events of that day: about the magnificently arrayed British legions and how they had massed for a grand assault on the American position, the green-coated dragoons and smart-stepping light infantrymen moving slowly at first and then more rapidly across the wide clearing, and then charging the hill with loud "Huzzas!" To both sides a British victory must have seemed inevitable. But then came a furious burst of fighting that suddenly, unaccountably, turned against the enemy and forced the arrogant Tarleton to troop back to Cornwallis in disgrace, minus some eight hundred men who had either been killed or taken prisoner. Much of the credit for halting the British charge belonged to the American general Daniel Morgan. Morgan, crippled with sciatica and barely able to sit a horse, had somehow transmitted to his men the same audacity, the same inexplicable courage, that had driven him to hazard all on a ground purposely chosen for its lack of escape routes, a spot where green recruits who had nowhere to run would inevitably be forced to stand and fight.

The battle over, Morgan turned and marched his men rapidly north for a rendezvous with the American commander-in-chief, crossing the Catawba ahead of the rising floodwaters. There is a story of how the two men, Morgan and Greene, and a third one now, the militia commander William L. Davidson, had met at Beatty's Ford and had been discussing defensive preparations when all at once, on a bank across the river, a numerous body of enemy cavalrymen appeared, and among them a man with spyglasses, thought to be Cornwallis himself. But the force of eight hundred American militiamen guarding the ford was enough temporarily to halt the British advance.

Early the next morning, while creating an elaborate diversion with one wing of his army, Cornwallis marched the main force four miles downstream to Cowan's Ford, a more suitable crossing. It was not yet full dawn when the British reached the water's edge. Cornwallis ordered his men into the still-rising stream even though the flickering campfires on the opposite bank warned him that the enemy was waiting. The American pickets, suddenly aroused, poured a "steady and galling fire" into the ranks of the British soldiers, who nonetheless came implacably on, lashed about by the current, some of them carried away rapidly downstream as the bullets hit, the others emerging cold and dripping and apparition-like along the slippery redclay bank. Out of the stream, and kneeling in good order, they immediately began to fire at the now-fleeing Americans, who had been thrown into a headlong retreat almost at the instant that their commander, General Davidson, was shot dead from his horse.

The British hurriedly assembled their forces and gave chase. After riding all morning through a driving rain Tarleton and his dragoons caught up with the wildly retreating militiamen at Torrence's Tavern, a popular way-station on the Salisbury road. Also at the tavern were dozens of refugees who, with their farm wagons and all their belongings, had set out to seek the protection of General Greene, and who squatted there in huddled and faceless masses, a crowd of men and women upon whom the British cavalrymen had suddenly fallen with slashing swords and cries of "Remember the Cowpens," striking with equal abandon at drunken soldiers, startled farmers, clothes trunks, bedticks, milk pails, chicken coops, butter churns, and lowing cattle.

About this same time General Greene and a small party of dragoons had ridden into Salisbury with hopes of raising another corps of militiamen and a cache of usable muskets. The general had been disappointed in both hopes and had left the town, so legend tells us, with nothing more than a small bag of coins, the life savings of Mrs. Elizabeth Steele, tavern mistress, who had been moved to pity while he and his men sat disconsolately at breakfast. Legend also tells us how Greene now quickly rejoined Morgan in time for the crossing of the Yadkin, how his by-now encyclopedic knowledge of the countryside, gained systematically and with great speed after his appointment as commander-in-chief of the southern armies, had convinced him that after a day of heavy rain his troops would have less than two days to put a second and perhaps more formidable river between themselves and the British.

The Americans finally got across on the evening of the second day, just ahead of their pursuers; and the British officers, who had ordered the burning of wagons and surplus supplies in order to speed their advance, were again forced to stand and wait, to bide their time, while far below them the thick wild current swirled ever higher. At length, baffled and frustrated by a three-day delay, Cornwallis swung his troops north toward the Shallow Ford, some forty miles distant, and after another five days of marching finally pushed his way across the river and again set out in rapid pursuit of the American armies.

During these same five days the Americans had moved even more rapidly on their own northward march across the red clay hills of the Carolina Piedmont, shrewdly drawing the British further and further from their main base of supplies, the rain still coming down and the men themselves half starved, half out of their clothes, forlorn, leaving behind them a trail of bloody footprints. In time they reached the banks of yet another swollen river, the Dan this time, and crossed over safely into Virginia while Cornwallis was again brought up short—was left to stand and gaze despairingly at the rising current while about him the Americans' last campfires flickered and died. Retiring to Hillsborough, the British general at once proclaimed the restoration of royal rule, and was busily seeking the aid of local Tories even as his foes, rested now and their ranks swollen with recruits, were recrossing the river and moving quickly to take up the high ground around Guilford Courthouse. On that ground they would face the British in one of the most savage battles of this or any other war, a battle that gained Cornwallis the field ("I never saw such fighting since God made me," he said) but with a victory only pyrrhic, his army having been reduced by almost a third while the American force had remained more or less intact. Greene's only regret was that he had had to rely too heavily on inexperienced

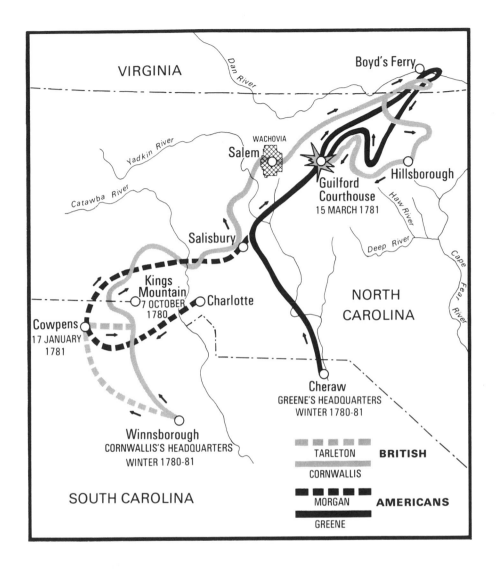

VIRGINIA

Dan River

Boyd's Ferry

Yadkin River

WACHOVIA
Salem

Guilford
Courthouse
15 MARCH 1781

Hillsborough

Haw River

Catawba River

Salisbury

Deep River

Cape Fear River

Kings
Mountain
7 OCTOBER
1780

Charlotte

NORTH
CAROLINA

Cowpens
17 JANUARY
1781

Cheraw
GREENE'S HEADQUARTERS
WINTER 1780-81

Winnsborough
CORNWALLIS'S HEADQUARTERS
WINTER 1780-81

TARLETON **BRITISH**
CORNWALLIS

MORGAN **AMERICANS**
GREENE

SOUTH CAROLINA

*From Cowpens to Guilford: For Lord Cornwallis, the long road to Yorktown
had begun with Banastre Tarleton's humiliating defeat at Cowpens. Cornwallis's subsequent pursuit of the Americans across the Carolina piedmont
yielded only slightly better results. The showdown clash at Guilford
Courthouse ended with the British general claiming victory but with one-
fourth of his men, including many experienced officers, now lost to him. In
Britain the parliamentary leader Charles James Fox lamented: "Another such
victory would destroy the British army"*

North Carolina militiamen, who, if they had stood their ground, might well have given the new republic a victory on the scale of Yorktown. "They left the most advantageous position I ever saw, without scarcely firing a gun," he said.[1]

More than a month before the Battle of Guilford Courthouse, Cornwallis and his army had crossed the Yadkin with every expectation of a quick mop-up action that would reestablish royal government in North Carolina and all but assure the early conquest of Virginia. The British troops had come up through Rowan County along the future Wilkesboro road and then swung northeast through the present-day Mocksville and Farmington communities. On their last day before crossing the river they raided a farm belonging to the patriot leader Jonathan Hunt, destroying most of the buildings on the place and taking the old man prisoner. By the morning or early afternoon of 8 February they were across the Shallow Ford, followed at some distance by a little corps of American cavalrymen under Captain Joseph Graham. Cornwallis may never even have known about the skirmish between these Americans and some of his rear-guard stragglers. Graham had not made bold to pursue the British too far beyond the river, as he was under the impression that he was now in a country "reputed to be favorable to the British."[2] Late that afternoon, with six prisoners and a dead Hessian to his credit, Graham hurriedly recrossed the Shallow Ford and united his force with the newly formed Pickens militia, a body of some seven hundred men who had reassembled after the battle of Cowan's Ford and had later banded together under the standard of the gentlemanly South Carolinian, Andrew Pickens.

And so Cornwallis marched on, confident, with brave accoutrements, his 3,000-man army growing stronger now in spite of his overextended supply line. Up from the Shallow Ford he came, halting overnight at "Lindsay's Plantation," a place since lost to history, and moving on into Bethania late the next morning. Bethania was like a Roman holiday for the British soldiers. Had Cornwallis deliberately sought out this town because it had thrown in with the rebels? Was his purpose in camping there primarily to harass the citizens for their anti-British sentiments? This was a common belief for many years in

Bethania, and perhaps not a mistaken belief at that. We know that Bethania was anything but a typical Moravian community in its attitude toward the war, and its apostasy could hardly have been news to Cornwallis and his soldiers. In any case, if reprisal had been no part of their thoughts, they might have more logically camped in Bethabara or Salem, either of which lay more directly in their line of march.

The Reverend Eli W. Caruthers, writing at a time when memories of the war were still fresh, accurately described Bethania as a town seething with revolutionary ferment. Caruthers believed that most other Moravians "were rather in favor of the British," more so in Salem than elsewhere. "But in Bethany, now called Hoozertown[3] . . . they were almost to a man, in favor of independence."[4]

The British officers and soldiers immediately took over the village and began ordering everybody around. A cold rain fell steadily all that afternoon and evening, yet without subduing the boisterous spirits of these lords of misrule, who thronged the streets, tavern, barnlots, and even the houses, tracking alien mud and the filth of many a nightly bivouac into the neatly swept Moravian halls—all of this while outside great fires roared and huge cauldrons bubbled merrily, the shouts and laughter of 3,000 hungry soldiers mingling with the moos and cackles of doomed farm animals. Before the day was out the Britishers had butchered more than sixty head of cattle, not to mention uncounted numbers of sheep, chickens, and geese, and had sent to Bethabara for one hundred gallons of whisky, three hundred pounds of bread, and "all the meal that was ready." By dark everyone must have been quite drunk, "so royally drunk," Caruthers says, "that five hundred sober and resolute men could have taken the whole without any difficulty."[5] It was about this time perhaps that one of the British officers, maybe Cornwallis himself, got the idea of forcing the men of the community to profess obeisance to their British overlords. As Caruthers tells the story:

It was determined to make all the men in the village drink the health of King George; and his lordship, if he had anything more in view than amusement, probably thought, that if he did not get them in this way fairly committed, he would at least mortify their feelings, and thus punish them a little for their rebellious spirit. So, having got the leading ones together, he, or one of his officers, holding a bottle in his hand, told them that they must all drink the health of King George; and he began with old Hoozer, who was a leading character among them. Having no good will to the king, and not wishing to act hypocritically, when the bottle was presented, he refused; but the officer told him that if he did not he would run his sword through him. This was placing the honest old Dutchman in a predicament which he did not expect, and for which he was not prepared. As the only alternative was death or compliance, he reached out his hand very reluctantly for the bottle, and, as he drew it slowly towards his mouth, said "Vell den, here is to de helt of King Chorge." Then putting the bottle to his mouth, and letting it gurgle a little, but taking care not to swallow any of its contents, he handed it back; but as he did so, he turned his head over the other shoulder, and said to his friends, though in a voice which was heard by them alone, "And tam him, he is nutting de better for dat." Encouraged by his example, the rest all drank the health of King George in the same way, and all felt, no doubt, when it was done, that he was "nothing the better for that." His lordship, unconscious, we suppose, of the trick that had been played upon him, or upon his master at home, gave orders at night for leaving next morning.[6]

The hero of this story might have been the same George Hauser who had once defied the wishes of his church by marrying a non-Moravian and also by actively supporting the cause of independence. Or it might have been his brother Michael, a justice of the peace and tax collector who apparently had been equally outspoken in behalf of the common cause.

Earlier in the day, Cornwallis had issued an order for a fresh supply of horses, twenty of them, all to be ready promptly at six o'clock the next morning. The Brethren explained that they could not possibly furnish so many horses on such short notice. The British officers responded with threats. "Everything was in the greatest confusion and no one knew what to do, for all houses were filled with officers and their servants," said the Reverend Mr. Ernst. "At dusk a second written order was received . . . with repetition of the threats." The minister, who had spent the evening alternately trying to arrange for the delivery of the horses and explaining to Cornwallis that they could not be found, had just gotten back to his house when a British subaltern appeared at the door. The man had a threatening look and a wild plan: he would seize Brother Ernst and hold him hostage until all demands had been strictly met. The plan came to naught when some of the other officers, including the chief commissary of the infantry, intervened in the minister's behalf. Yet the British would have their horses nonetheless, and the Brethren eventually produced seventeen of the requested number. Even at that Cornwallis was only eleven to the good, since six of the seventeen "had been taken secretly from the English teamsters."[7]

It was now Saturday, 10 February, and still raining. The march began at 7:00 A.M. The dragoons who made up the advance guard were already in Salem, nine miles away, before the rear guard had left Bethania. For six hours the army trooped down the soggy lane through Old Town, as Bethabara was already coming to be known, two guards posted at the tavern and another at the stillhouse. Lorenz Bagge, the Bethabara diarist and minister, found little else to report, noting only that "Lord Cornwallis and several gentlemen were pleased to dismount; several of us waited upon him and he was friendly and seemed satisfied."[8]

The earl undoubtedly assumed that he was again among friends, an assumption neither wholly true nor wholly false. The hope that these "united provinces" would some day resume their place in the empire cannot have been entirely absent from the thoughts of such men as Traugott Bagge and Frederic William Marshall. But even in the "Tory towns" of Bethabara and Salem an uncertain wind of freedom was blowing. Caruthers tells the story of the Salem cook who was "such an inveterate Whig, that neither threats nor persuasion could prevail on him to prepare anything for Cornwallis and his staff to eat. . . ."

"Marshall . . . used his influence," Caruthers said, "but in vain. The officers tried coaxing him, but he told them to go home, and stay there, and not be coming here to kill our people, destroy our property, and make us slaves to King George. They then threatened, in an angry tone, to cut him down with their swords, but not one bite would the dogged old Dutchman get for them."[9]

Whether this tale is literally true is of no great moment. That such stories were told at all gives us some clue as to the changing attitudes of the town. It is one of the very few clues we have. Even the persevering reader will find it hard to discover any obvious trends to this effect in the Moravian diaries. One might say that this shift in sentiment had begun to be discernible when the Moravian leaders began issuing stern anti-Tory proclamations in late 1780. Or he could argue in exactly the opposite vein: that these men were merely restating in a more emphatic manner their traditional appeal for neutrality, an appeal far more urgent now that British arms were momentarily in the ascendancy and the loyalist forces thus in a position to command more respect from wavering factions. The surprising thing is that there could have been any pro-American feeling at all in a town that had been so roughly handled by the liberty men.

The approach of the British army had only made matters worse in this respect. On the day before Cornwallis had crossed the Shallow Ford a gang of these roughhousing soldiers from the hollows of the Yadkin had descended on the town with a wild apocalyptic cry of freedom and a warning that anyone who was for the common cause "should now show it."[10] There were almost two hundred of them, all members of a Wilkes County militia unit on its way to join General Greene. What motivated this particular group of malefactors was something more than mere envy of the Moravians, or resentment of their military exemptions, something more even than the desire for food and drink and a big night on the town. These men, and their intemperate captain William Lenoir most of all, still blamed the Brethren for insisting on their legal rights in connection with the Mulberry Fields, the 9,000-acre Moravian-owned tract on which the town of Wilkesboro is now located. Probably most of them were recent squatters on that land. Lenoir, an easterner by birth, had settled there in 1774, apparently convinced of his right to do so even before the land had become the subject of confiscation talk. If convinced of it then, obviously he was all the more convinced of it now.

After the war the Moravians would seek clarification of their title (though they would already have sold the land) in the General Assembly, only to have this same Captain Lenoir, who by then would be president of the Senate, delay and finally kill a bill that would have permanently resolved the legal tangle.

Later the Brethren would appeal to the University of North Carolina's board of trustees, which had claim to all the land that had reverted to the state under wartime confiscation laws.[11]

Lenoir?

By then he would himself be a member of the board and would persuade his colleagues to rescind a resolution in which they had renounced all rights to the controversial tract. Then would ensue the long series of legal battles, already mentioned, during which the Brethren would twice have their title confirmed by the state Supreme Court.

But in this cold grim February of 1781 their legal rights mattered little and their moral rights not at all. Lenoir, who had fought in General Rutherford's 1776 campaign against the Cherokees and had been wounded at Kings Mountain, swaggered into town declaring that all Moravians "were his enemies." We see him in half light, hand on saber, his skinny wild face torn by a yellowish grin, a man not yet in his thirtieth year, ordering the Brethren to submit or suffer. Just do as he said and nobody would get hurt. Lenoir and his men "ate and drank as they pleased," commandeered oats, meal, salt, corn, pottery ware, half an ox, all the "public lead," huge quantities of brandy, and, in short, took "whatever came to hand."

"After we had had much trouble with them, and had felt the Power of Darkness, they left about ten o'clock at night, with a show of politeness. . . . Prior to leaving, several of them went into the town, represented themselves as Tories and tried to lead the Brethren to join them, but they did not succeed, for the Saviour gave our Brethren grace to speak cautiously, and protected them from harm."[12]

The next morning they were back. No worship services could be held and there was much trouble at the stillhouse and tavern, "much cursing, abuse, and harsh threats so that we feared for our lives and our property."[13]

It was the same almost everywhere. In Friedberg the tales of violence continued to mount, among them a report that "the elder Greter had been badly treated, that he had been beaten, dragged about by the hair, and trampled upon."

"We were the more grieved," said the Friedberg diarist, "as we heard that he had given no reason for such treatment."[14]

The captain strode in, hand on saber, declaring that all Moravians "were his enemies"

From Friedberg also came the troubling story of Martin Walk. Walk was said to have been seized by men in British uniform, declared an enemy of the land, and taken away prisoner. Later reports made it clear that his abductors were actually Americans. There was nothing against Walk but an old and discredited rumor to the effect that he was part of a "combination" which presumably had designs on the new Whig government, but perhaps in these times no other evidence was needed. Walk would eventually escape and return home to find his daughter Sarah dead from smallpox.

Helpless against the bullying tactics of Lenoir and the Wilkes crowd, the people of Salem had sent out an urgent distress call to General Greene and the American army. Two Moravian emissaries, the saddler Charles Holder and the assistant storekeeper George Bibighaus, had ridden with all haste to the Abbotts Creek neighborhood, where Greene was now quartered, and delivered a petition requesting armed protection for the town of Salem and reminding the general that "Tho' this Town was but inhabited in the Years 1772 & 1773, which was 2 & 3 years before the breaking out of this War, & consequently is but in its Infancy, not containing quite 20 Dwelling houses, & scarce one hundred grown persons, Men & Women included, besides the difficulty of all Beginners that we owe great Part of our Stock in Trade & our Houses to others, we have never been behindhand with any part of the County but rather unsupported by the County Commissioner the whole Weight of providing for the Troops is always fallen upon us."[15]

The Brethren also informed him that they had always acted in a spirit of "Chearfullness" when called upon to provide for the needs of American soldiers and protested the evil treatment they had gotten in return. They especially protested "the unreasonable Treatment we just now received of a couple of hundred Militia from another County, come here under pretence of going to join Yr Excys Army, but far from that seeming to have much Time on their Hands, and continually exacting new Quantities of Brandy, Meat, Bread, Flower, Corn, Salt, pressing of Horses & shoeing their own, with horrid Imprecations, striking the People, coining of Stories, & threatening not to leave this Place, before they have killed a

Number of us, besides many pretences to pick a Quarrel or invade People's Properties."[16]

The general replied that he was unable to provide such aid "as the English must be already in our towns." And it was true. "When they arrived we were worrying about them."[17] The horse soldiers arrived about ten that morning, the rest of the army following in irregular order. It was quite late in the day before the last of the rear guard passed through town and out along what is now Waughtown Street toward the Friedland settlement. During much of the afternoon Cornwallis and his entourage, which included the royal governor-in-exile Josiah Martin, relaxed at the home of Traugott Bagge—or rather in the two-story apartment which Bagge at that time still called home.[18] The welcoming party was small and discreet, consisting only of the Brethren Bagge and Marshall.

The records tell us little of what happened that afternoon. But we are hardly to suppose that these two men, who had been forced for so long to keep a tactful silence, would have let these brief hours slip by without in some way paying homage to the old order. Perhaps they would have stood there, these men and their guests, in the solemn half-light of that winter afternoon, and again raised their glasses to the health of the king. No doubt there would have been much talk of the good times before the war, and it may even be that one of them would have thoughtfully echoed Thomas Jefferson's poignant comment: "We could have been a free and a great people together."

The next day there was a new mood in Salem. The ones going to church must have noticed it—must have noticed the profound and unexpected atmosphere of calm that hung over the town, must have noticed that for once there were no obnoxious soldiers in their path, no wild and threatening laughter, no clamorous demands for requisitions. Throughout the afternoon and evening and on into the next day the town was quiet, the streets empty.

And then again came the cry of liberty: again the shouts of drunken soldiery, the perverse and accusing stares, again the sound of riotous midnight revelry, with people banging at the doors, shouting, lurking darkly about mysterious corners, peering in the windows, rattling the shutters, yelping,

A toast to the old order and perhaps an echo of Thomas Jefferson's poignant comment: "We could have been a free and a great people together"

howling, laughing. And maybe one of them exclaiming, "Who goes there?" And the answer in the dark: "No friend of King George."

And there was a new complaint this time: if the people of Salem and Bethabara had not been secretly aiding the enemy, how had they managed to escape the kind of brutal punishment meted out to Bethania? The answer was that the British had not camped overnight in either of those towns and consequently had had less time to abuse the citizens and make peremptory demands. Not that Salem had entirely escaped such exactions. In that town the British soldiers and their camp followers had confiscated nine head of cattle from the tavern lot, relieved Dr. Bonn of forty pounds sterling, pressed brandy and oxen, and stolen all the wash off the Single Brethren's clothesline.

In Friedland, a Moravian settlement founded ten years earlier by a group of immigrants from Broadbay, Maine, there was worse trouble. Here again the British set down their overnight encampment. Here again there were wholesale requisitions, threats, beatings. The people living near the camp "lost nearly all their forage and cattle. All sorts of excesses were committed by wandering parties seeking food. They forced their way into the Schoolhouse also, and Br. and Sr. Heinzmann gave so long as they had anything. Toward nine o'clock there came six or eight men, to whom they gave their last bit of bread and meat. In spite of all Br. Heinzmann's statements they fiercely insisted upon having more, and went through the provision closet taking anything they could find. His wife was in bed with such a pain in her back that she could not rest, but now she got up. When he tried to leave the house to call for help they thrust a naked bayonet at his breast, ready to stab or shoot."[19]

All of this might have been offered as evidence that Bethania had not been singled out for special treatment, that Salem and Bethabara had not been spared simply because of their alleged Tory sympathies. But there was something else that was harder to explain: Bagge's overly gracious reception of Cornwallis and his party. As a result of that two- or three-hour visit the Salem Brethren soon found themselves on the receiving end of "all sorts of alarming reports." Most alarming of all was a rumor that Major Joseph Winston, a man once friendly to the

Moravians, had been convinced by the Cornwallis episode that they were all traitors and was even now marching north "to punish the town."[20]

The town waited, uncertain. And then about noon the next day the major did appear, all smiles, dining with a fellow officer at the tavern and giving no one cause for further concern. "They brought no men, having dismissed their companies ten miles from here, and they were very friendly."[21]

But with Winston's departure the "powers of darkness" were quick to resume command. "That the fiend had planned the overthrow of our towns may be assumed from the lies that sprang up, saying that Salem ought to be burned because it had encouraged the British army to burn Bethania." The fiend came not only in the familiar guise of the Wilkes militia but in many others: malicious refugees from General Greene's army, random groups of pressmen and foragers from the Pickens militia, some two hundred cavalrymen from Lincoln, Rowan, and Mecklenburg counties (though the officers in charge of these men were "very polite"), and, most troublesome of the lot, a band of freebooters under Major Micajah Lewis, a Continental officer who spoke "as though the destruction of our town had been determined." It was primarily through the offices of Lewis and his gang that one of the Brethren "was stopped on the street [and] his coat . . . taken off his back and stolen" and also because of them that "hardly one house remained unrobbed." These men had put together a list of men "whom they particularly wanted to injure" and sought "every opportunity to find evidence of treason, or of correspondence with the British, so that they might destroy us on that pretext."[22]

At the top of the list was Traugott Bagge. In all likelihood Bagge would not have survived this latest onslaught except for the timely intervention of such sympathetic American officers as Captain Joseph Graham. Graham and his cavalry company had stopped off in Salem one afternoon while marching from the Shallow Ford to Guilford Courthouse. Bagge saw to it that they were "promptly and politely" served at the tavern and then solicited their help in fending off the Wilkes crowd. Some of this mountain horde had appeared suddenly and begun to ransack the community store while Graham and his men were still at dinner. The captain "immediately went to these marauders and ordered them to desist." But they just stood there looking at him with a mixture of reproach, disappointment, incomprehension, as though a little hurt by his inability to understand the justice of their cause. They explained to the captain that "the Moravians were all Tories" (and Graham, of course, had once been convinced of that himself), that they themselves had been victimized by Tories and that therefore they had a right "to make themselves whole." Graham was unmoved. Ordering his own men up from the tavern, he forced the Wilkes terrorists to put back what they had stolen and clear out of town.[23]

After that everything is a blur: Bagge being pinned to the wall by a militiaman flashing a "bare sabre" and threatening to cut him in two, Bagge being rescued at the last moment by a group of friendly officers and then almost immediately being accosted by a man with a loaded flintlock. There was talk of how the assailant repeatedly rammed the gun into the merchant's chest, screaming curses at him and interrogating him about his tête-à-tête with Cornwallis, and how at the critical juncture the officers again rushed in to the rescue. Later that same week another group of soldiers, maybe twenty of them in all, appeared at Bagge's door, armed and belligerent, and forced their way into his living room. What was there between him and Cornwallis anyway? Had there been some kind of arms deal? Wasn't it true that he had been supplying the British with guns and powder ever since the outbreak of the war? This time it was the playfulness of Bagge's children that diverted the men from their chief aim, which was perhaps not to kill but only to maim and maybe even only to frighten the merchant, and most of all to strip his home of everything that would bear carrying off.

The next evening two officers moved in to protect Bagge and his family. But who was to protect the rest of the town? John Frederick Peter, the Salem minister who had recently succeeded Bishop Graff as keeper of the congregational diary, reported that "two or three of the band, having eaten and drunk all they desired, roamed through the town all night, frightening now this and now that family, making them empty chests and show their contents, saying they were 'looking for powder which the English had left here.' As they also asked about hard money, fine shirts, handkerchiefs, and the like, it was sufficiently clear what they really wanted, and much was stolen, and it was a wonder of God that Salem was not totally plundered."[24]

During that same week the General Assembly had twice been on the point of rescinding the Brethren's right to refuse military induction. The idea was first proposed at a time when the House lacked a quorum and could not vote and was later defeated with the help of legislators who had initially been in favor of the motion but who had changed their minds in the interim. This, however, was not the last the Brethren were to hear of such schemes.

The week also brought an offer of help from Major Winston, who apparently had become alarmed over events in Salem and had written to ask Bagge what might be done to restore order. The offer had come at a particularly opportune moment (though nothing more was heard of it) because the Brethren had just now fallen prey to yet another gang of boisterous militiamen. These were members of a 400-man mounted force commanded by Colonel John Preston. Most of Preston's troops had camped at Bethabara and behaved in an orderly enough fashion; others had drifted on into Salem, where they may have hoped to find a more suitable welcome. The men kept the town up to all hours, and next morning "had to be entertained with organ-playing and other interests." And then came Colonel Preston himself, he with an "unusually hearty" greeting and a thousand assurances that "nothing . . . suffered from his soldiers should go unpunished."[25]

But let the diarist himself describe a typical series of events:

Feb. 23. In the afternoon other small parties came, returning from the army or from other service. They demanded food and drink, and some of them went further. Some of those who remained over night behaved well, but some of Captain Lapp's company were antagonistic to us, though they became somewhat milder after attending the evening meeting.

Feb. 24. The men from Captain Lapp's company sneaked away, after securing brandy; the others left with courtesy. During the morning an American *flag of truce* passed, led by Surgeon Richard Pindell and Lieutenant Samuel Hanson of the Maryland troops; and a British *flag of truce*, led by Dr. Jackson and Surgeon Stewart of the 71st

Regiment. They were on their way from the Cowpens, in South Carolina, to their respective armies. These gentlemen looked over the town, with approval, and went on after breakfast. At the request of the former group some money was given them on General Morgan's account. Colonel Preston sent a soldier back to the doctor, as he had carelessly shot off his thumb with his own gun. The Baptist minister, Hill, and Captain Holbert, of the Dan River settlement, came on a visit. The former and Colonel Winston had planned that Mr. Hill and one or two Justices should stay here to aid us when passing soldiers made unjust demands on us, but he could not remain, for the small-pox, which was beginning to creep about on Dan River, was breaking out on him. . . .

The Saviour sent us a quiet evening, so that we might refresh our souls in His Holy Sacrament.

Feb. 26. Things fell again into their usual channel, but not so badly . . . Br. [Johannes] Reutz' great-coat and Br. Bonn's horse were returned, both the worse for use. [Some of the militiamen] were tame in their manner, but next morning,

Feb. 27, they could not refrain from taking off various things on all sorts of pretexts. All day parties came and went, eating and drinking *at public expense*. Four, who said they belonged to General Pickens, pressed iron at the store and work at the smithy. . . .

Feb. 28. The Pickens men stole three hats from Br. Reutz; the others followed their example. Both parties pressed bread from the baker, without paying for it, to take it away with them,—so it happens every day. . . .[26]

And then the Wilkes militia was back: a glint of steel, a crescendo of whoops and hollers, a tableau of gaunt whiskery faces, flesh and metal both glimmering in the abrupt harsh flare of hastily lit candles. "From some things that were said they seem to be ashamed of their former behaviour, but they were little better this time." The marauders moved from tavern to Brothers House and back to the tavern, and toward the shank of the evening barged into the distillery with swords drawn and "committed all sorts of excesses."[27]

This time their merriment was cut short by the arrival of Colonel William Campbell, one of the heroes of Kings Mountain. Campbell, the Virginia officer who had been in charge of the Bethabara Tory hunt the previous fall, "gave emphatic warning to Captain Lenoir of Wilkes, concerning the bad behaviour of himself and his men"[28] and promised to provide the town with the protection General Greene had been forced to deny. A guard detail arrived five days later and was withdrawn the next.

It was now well into March, and the two armies were rapidly closing ranks for the climactic battle of Guilford Courthouse. And so it happened that even on the most uneventful of days there was a constant movement of troops through Salem, a constant drain on Moravian stores and, in the diaries, a constantly recurring note to the effect that "today the confusion began again."

The first news of the fighting came by way of a Hessian rifleman who had "run away at the beginning of [the] battle, and did not know how it had ended."[29] The next day the Brethren learned that Greene was in full retreat, though they could not yet have known that the battle was, in its net result, an important strategic victory for the Americans.

And then there were more troop movements, more fleeing and wounded soldiers. On 21 March, almost a week after the battle, they received from Major John Armstrong, brother to the colonel, a letter "containing a friendly warning not to send help to the British hospital." Later the major seemed most gratified to learn that they had sent "nothing except rags for the use of the wounded."[30]

But the story is not yet quite told, for it was during this period that the Moravians began to experience what many of the American colonists had been complaining about for years: the forced quartering of soldiers in their homes. Parliament had required the colonial assemblies and hence the colonists themselves to provide lodging for the royal troops—in taverns, in deserted buildings, and, when these were lacking, in occupied dwellings—and, in addition, to keep the soldiers well supplied with beer and rum. This was one of the many irritants that had led to the Revolution, and was directly responsible for our Third Amendment guarantee against forced quartering. To be sure, it was never to become a great and abiding issue on a par with the tax controversy; however, it was an issue of profound concern, and one on which there should have been some semblance of agreement between the colonists and parliamentary leaders, many of whom had long been agitated by similar constitutional questions. Some of these leaders, the Old Whigs whose moment of power had passed, men like the eloquent Edmund Burke and the elder Pitt, had long been sympathetic to American complaints and had often urged conciliatory treatment. Pitt most of all would have understood their grievances with respect to the quartering matter. His great speech on the rights of privacy is still quoted by civil libertarians and old-fashioned constitutionalists alike: "The poorest man may in his cottage bid defiance to all the force of the Crown. It may be frail; its roof may shake; the wind may blow through it; the storms may enter, the rain may enter,—but the King of England cannot enter; all his forces dare not cross the threshold of the ruined tenement!"

It was not so in America. Here the king's forces entered at will, in Bethania as in Boston, and so for that matter did the Americans when it suited their whim or when the need for housing became acute. In Wachovia the burden appears to have fallen mainly on Salem and Bethabara, but it was not unusual for any of the Moravian communties to be suddenly overrun with homeless soldiers. One night in February of 1781 the Friedberg diarist counted up to twenty-six soldiers lodged in many of the homes in his community.

In this as in most other matters relating to the war the Brethren sought to cooperate fully with the military authorities, the idea being that they had rather "give them a meadow than have them take one."[31] One of the major concerns was how to keep from lodging the soldiers in the farm buildings and stillhouses, "for from the congregational standpoint it would work harm to our young men to be mixed with the soldiers, and from the economic standpoint it would be disadvantageous in that it would permit the soldiers to set the price on food which supports the entire town." The Brethren preferred to empty whole houses and turn them over to the military rather than allow the soldiers to lodge among the families or in the choir houses, where they would "endanger the spiritual life of our people." And yet for all that the soldiers quite often lived "at discretion in many places."[32]

The Brethren treated everybody about the same: Americans, British, and deserters from both armies. And they provided these soldiers with something infinitely more valuable than food or lodging—desperately needed medical attention in a backcountry where doctors were as scarce as dancing bears. Quite early in the year 1781, twenty-two American cavalrymen, sick and wounded, were transported to Salem from the battlefields of South Carolina, so that they might enjoy the services of Dr. Jacob Bonn and his apprentice Joseph Dixon. All but four of these men somehow managed to squeeze into a 16-by-13 log hut built recently for the Salem night watchman Heinrich Zillman. Another group, some thirty strong, arrived later in the month and found lodging with the tanner Peter Yarrell. Though not badly hurt, all of these men had been sent to Salem expressly to recover their health. Not long after that the Brethren emptied a two-story house at what is now Main and Bank Streets to make room for the Continental Hospital. The "hospital," a great accumulation of cots, bandages, primitive surgical instruments, and bleeding and armless men propped up in creaky wagons, moved on after an overnight stay, presumably to seek out safer quarters in Virginia. Smaller groups of wounded men limped in almost daily, and about this same time the town of Friedberg was struck by a smallpox epidemic even more virulent than the one that had struck Salem two years earlier. The threat of the spreading contagion would force Salem to begin an extensive inoculation program immediately after the Easter holidays.

All of this would have its effect on Dr. Bonn. Now forty-eight years old, Bonn had apparently outlived a youthful reputation for untidiness and licentiousness. "We have heard that he liked to be among the sisters," John Ettwein had once written of him, "and annoyed them by paying them long visits when their husbands were not at home."[33] This was not the Jacob Bonn that Salem knew in 1781. Next to Traugott Bagge and possibly Frederic Marshall he was perhaps the man most often looked to for guidance in legal and political affairs, having served in recent years as a justice of the peace and also as chairman of the county court. The local committee of safety had stripped him of most of his authority, but only for political reasons, and no one seems to have doubted his competence either as a "public man," one of the few in eighteenth-century Wachovia, or as a physician, a job which at the time demanded both the instincts of an artist and the skills of a scientist. Within a few months, though, Dr. Bonn would die of a stroke, probably worn down from overwork, and Wachovia would be left only with his inexperienced apprentice Joseph Dixon. Dixon had been assigned to take up the study of medicine mainly because he seemed to lack aptitude for anything else. Unhappily for Salem he seemed equally ungifted at the practice of medicine; some may even have thought it providential that Dr. Bonn did not die until most of the military activities in the Wachovia area had ceased.

Dr. Adelaide Fries believed that the willingness of the Moravians to provide the American armies with what was then regarded as expert medical attention was one of the things that "gradually turned sentiment in their favor."[34] She undoubtedly had a point. But there was no real softening of attitude, or at least none that was apparent, until later that year when members of the state assembly met in Salem and had a chance to investigate for themselves the good reports that had drifted back from American military commanders.

In their response to the varied demands made on them the Moravians betrayed their usual flair for careful planning, a typically Germanic trait that seems to require order above all things. Obviously uncertain as to how much quartering would be expected of them in the future, and tired of running the Brothers and Sisters out of their homes every time a new detachment of soldiers came through, they had erected near Salem Tavern an ammunition depot and a two-room soldiers' barracks described in the Moravian Records as a "house for poor travelers." But neither of the buildings would long serve its intended purpose. By the spring of 1781 the two armies had moved far beyond Wachovia, and with their departure came an abrupt end to the violence and to the almost constant demand for bed space and battle supplies.

This was not yet the real calm of peace. Yorktown was still some months distant and the official declaration of peace would have to wait until the spring of 1783. The unrest and violence and pillaging would continue in many parts of the state and even to some extent in Wachovia. But the Moravians would no longer experience on an almost daily basis the horrors that had plagued them for the last five years or more, and North Carolina would no longer be an active theater of war.

After the dubious British victory at Guilford Courthouse Cornwallis's army staggered southeast toward Wilmington and further disillusionments, Cornwallis himself having given up all thought of subduing North Carolina until Virginia had been brought to heel. He now believed—he who had more reason for believing it than anyone else—that the state through which he was now marching was "of all the provinces in America, the most difficult to attack . . . on account of its great extent and of the numberless rivers and creeks and the total want of interior navigation."[35]

From the Tories he got none of the help he had expected. These once-militant allies would drift in to camp, shake hands, congratulate the general on his recent "victory," and then hasten back to their farms. Three times during his invasion of the state Cornwallis announced the restoration of royal authority, but nowhere did these "sunshine loyalists" rise up in sufficient numbers or with sufficient dedication to hold the ground after he and his troops had moved on beyond the next hill or treeline.

And so with the flowering of another Carolina spring the people of Wachovia could at last shake off the weariness of this long war and proclaim in triumph what they had once proclaimed in despair: "Thou art a strength to the poor, a strength to the needy in his distress, a refuge from the storm, a shadow from the heat."

In July the Salem Brethren learned that their town was to be the meeting place for the autumn session of the North Carolina Assembly. Towns usually sought this honor; the Moravians had not. "Our hope is in the Lord, Who will help us," said the Bethabara diarist when he heard of the plans.[36]

In spite of this reaction, which we can be certain was fairly typical of the Moravian attitude, the Brethren would inevitably prepare for the event with an infinite amount of detail. Among the do's and don'ts: the tradesmen would sell no whisky or other strong drink to a Negro "even when he has hard money, without a written order from his master"; they would do no work on Sunday as that would "give great offence"; would refrain from selling bread as cheaply to their visitors as to members of the congregation; and when asked to change a gold coin would "give as little silver as possible, for we anticipate a scarcity of silver in the town." The women of the homes where the legislators were to stay would keep their guests in fresh clothing, either by washing it themselves or by gathering it up and explaining that it was to be taken to the washerwoman and then taking it instead to the Sisters' quarters, where it would be done up with great care as though a professional washer-woman had indeed had charge of the matter. As a special concession, they would hold only public worship services while the legislators were in town and, when attendance justified it, would recite the litany in English. Above all, the Brothers and Sisters would take care "that their bearing toward the Assemblymen may be brave, polite and friendly."[37]

They balked only at the idea of converting the town *Saal*[38] into a legislative chamber. Instead, they offered the governor, Alexander Martin, who had come to discuss arrangements, the stillhouse garret, "which is light and roomy," and an adjoining compartment. Neither the governor nor the legislators seem to have had any complaints about their three-week stay, and when the time was up and a quorum still unattained, they quickly voted to return for their January session. Among the Brethren the idea was no more popular this time than before, and Bagge went before the group to explain their position. The members "were told . . . that we preferred not to have the Assembly meet here, on account of the interruption of work in our shops, but if they decided on this town we would show all honor to our officials, and take the best care of them that we could."[39]

Actually the two sessions proved to be extremely beneficial to the Wachovia settlements. This was true even though assembly leaders were unable to muster a quorum for either meeting. It did not matter so much that some of the members "who do not like us"[40] lodged outside of town; the majority responded to Moravian hospitality in a spirit of friendship and understand-ing. One result became evident at the legislature's April session, when there was quick approval of a bill that finally ended most of the long controversy over Moravian land rights.

One night during the November meeting there came word that a band of Tories was on the way to arrest members of the assembly. The men repaired to Brother Marshall's apartment to wait out the alarm, which quickly subsided after the "Tories" were found to be nothing more than a gang of horse thieves. But the gathering did not break up till dawn. After serving his guests "a hot drink and cold cake" Marshall undertook a lengthy discussion of Moravian principles, answering "many modest questions"[41] about the history of the church and in the end dispelling any doubts these men may have had about the Brethren or about their loyalty to the new government.

Later Marshall had this to say about the legislators and their reaction to the Moravian worship services: "Our music and singing had a great effect on them, and they listened with wonder and respect. An old, gray-haired gentleman came to me expressly before leaving and said that he had always heard that we were a religious people, which was largely the reason that he had made the long trip to come here, but it had far surpassed his expectations. He was convinced that God was in our midst, and if he could do anything for us in the Assembly, personally or by his influence, he would do it gladly."[42]

9

"Peace Be within Thy Walls"

Across a wide mist-hung greensward from which night was already fading streamed a solemn and unspeaking mass of Moravian worshippers. There must have been at least a hundred and fifty of them, the whole population of the town, the men and boys in knee breeches and buckled shoes and open collarless jackets, and the women in linen caps and freshly laundered dresses—rusts, oranges, and pale blues—all moving quite rapidly and silently across Salem Square and up the steps to the *Gemein Haus*, where at any moment now the minister would greet them with the message for which all had been waiting:

"The Lord is risen!"

And the congregation responding:

"The Lord is risen indeed!"

As always, it was a message of hope, triumph, comfort, joy, a message also of great solemnity and peace, and this time with the reality of peace to match. Less than twenty-four hours earlier, during the celebration of the Great Sabbath, the Salem Brethren had unexpectedly received news of the British capitulation and the preliminary signing of the peace treaty: the first real asssurance that "rest will again be possible in this land."[1] And so we can imagine with what emotion they had risen on this Easter morning to celebrate the ultimate mystery of their faith: death, burial, and resurrection.

In Revolutionary times the sunrise service was already an old tradition with the Moravians, having developed out of an impromptu ceremony held some fifty years earlier on a hillside near the village of Herrnhut. The custom had persisted in the New World in spite of a superstitious and sometimes hostile neighbors. When Bethabara was still the chief town in Wachovia, the word had spread that the Brethren rose before dawn each Easter and trooped up Manakes Hill to their graveyard on God's Acre, and there opened the graves and wakened the dead with their trumpets, whereupon all of them, the quick and the dead alike, presumably turned as one and trooped back down the hill through the cool green April morning.

In the years since then the superstitions had faded and many of these same neighbors had been won over to the unique Moravian custom. In 1777 some one hundred and fifty "strangers" (non-Moravians) had gathered in Salem for the sunrise service, and there undoubtedly would be numerous others this year. But at this early hour, before the sun was quite up, the Brethren and Sisters would have the company of no one but themselves, all of them sitting quietly, reverently, in the dimly lit *Gemein Haus*, the band playing solemnly at first and then triumphantly,

> Hail, all hail, victorious Lord and Saviour,
> Thou has burst the bonds of death. . .

And the minister saying,
"The Lord is risen!"
And so back out into the bird-loud dawn and up the green hill to God's Acre where, hats in hand, the "strangers" would be waiting. The sun would have burst into view just as they approached the burial ground, the mists fading rapidly now, the coves and hollows and oak forests flooded with sun and music both, the wind rising ever so faintly, and the worshippers still prayerful, still silent, once again left to stand and meditate on the mystery of time and the glory of God's great handiwork.

Two months later, in response to a resolution enacted by the North Carolina General Assembly, Governor Martin issued a proclamation urging the people of the state to set aside the fourth of July as a day "of solemn Thanksgiving to Almighty God, for the many most gracious interpositions of his providence manifested in a great & signal manner" on behalf of the new "American Empire."[2]

The proclamation apparently inspired nothing in the way of a modern Fourth of July celebration. There must have been very few celebrations of any kind. The only one of which we have record occurred in the Moravian settlements in Wachovia. The spirit of the occasion was best observed in Salem, where members of the congregation gathered quite early to the sound of trombones, sang the Te Deum and heard again the thunderous words of Psalm 46:

Come, behold the works of the Lord, what desolations he hath made in the earth.

He maketh wars to cease unto the end of the earth; he breaketh the bow, and cutteth the spear in sunder; he burneth the chariot in the fire.

Be still, and know that I am God: I will be exalted among the heathen, I will be exalted in the earth.

Early that afternoon the Brethren and Sisters reassembled for a traditional lovefeast, a simple meal consisting of coffee, tea or wine and sweetened bun, and patterned after the *Agape* or meal in common of the first Christians. And then came the signing of John Frederick Peter's "Psalm of Joy," a magnificent cantatalike ode compiled especially for Salem's first Independence Day celebration:

Peace is with us, Peace is with us
People of the Lord!
Peace is with us, Peace is with us
Hear the joyful word!

And so it went throughout much of the afternoon, the town throbbing with the sound of violin and cello and organ, with great shouts of peace and glorious song,

Full of joy our hearts are singing
And to our God thank off'rings bringing
For His great miracle of peace!

The celebration lasted on into the evening. The sun had gone down and the last glow of it was fading rapidly as "the congregation again assembled in the Saal, and the choir sang: *Praise be to Thee, Who sittest above the cherubim*." After the service the worshippers took to the streets, forming a circle in front of the *Gemein Haus* and moving solemnly up through the main part of town, their faces lit by the glow of the flickering tapers and the night echoing now with the "antiphonal song of two choirs." Then back to the *Gemein Haus*, where they formed another large circle and stood in great reverence while "all around there was silence, even the wind being still."[3]

But this brief hush of peace soon gave way to a new turbulence, a new and even more daring spirit of freedom. The veneer of civilization left over from colonial times had broken down with the last feverish years of the Revolution and with the new radicalism that had sprung up in its wake. The Anglican Church no longer enjoyed its ancient privileges, schools had been closed, courts all but suspended, laws left uncodified, and no newspaper had been printed in the state since 1778. Worse than any of this was the depressing state of political affairs. Homeless, broke, and uncertain of its standing, the General Assembly wandered from town to town like an itinerant peddler, full of the promise of its coming but with little prospect of delivering even on the little that might reasonably have been expected.

What was true of North Carolina was true in equal or greater measure of the entire nation. "The land itself, the people of property, commerce, public and private credit, the currency in circulation, all are laid waste and ruined," said Frederic William Marshall.[4] In the years between the signing of the peace treaty and the adoption of the 1787 Constitution, Congress presided over nothing more than the empty forms of government. There was as yet no federal principle, no binding compact that would bring into focus the common objectives of the states. And indeed the concept of states' rights, which was to plague the nation's leaders long after the Revolution and eventually plunge the country into an even more terrible war, was already making itself felt as a potent and divisive political force.

Surprisingly enough, the Moravians had emerged from the Revolution and ensuing turmoil in much better shape, psychologically and even financially, than their neighbors. They had somehow escaped bankruptcy in spite of the depredations and violence of the closing years of the war, in spite of an uncertain currency, in spite of the continuing demand for requisitions, and they were again buying and

"All around there was silence, even the wind being still"

selling with their usual industry and frugality. "In other places no stores had been reopened," Marshall said, "so there was good trade in our store, in the pottery, which had again secured glazing, and in the tannery, where there was a stock of leather."[5] Because of this and possibly also because the nation had now more or less returned to a hard-money standard, the congregation soon made up all of its wartime losses and by the end of the 1783 budget year could even boast a degree of profit.

"With great thankfulness," said the *Aufseher Collegium*, "we saw that our Lord has given us very much during the last year."[6]

Throughout these years the Moravians had preserved and would continue to preserve much that was central to their heritage. To a very great extent the Brethren would hold to the old disciplines and rituals, the old authorities, and, yes, even the old aloofness—would continue to do so on into the next century. And to nothing would they cling more stubbornly than their faith. In the opinion of one author, no other denomination had so successfully resisted "the dry, inconstant winds of war and eighteenth-century rationalism."[7] Yet even the Moravians had changed—were bound to change—as royal rule gave way to a brawling backcountry democracy.

The first sure sign of change had been evident as early as the spring of 1778, when the Single Brethren struck for higher pay. It had become even more evident when the Brethren, yielding to the importunities of their good friend Governor Martin and other officials, began to feel less inhibited about participating in public affairs[8]—when, for instance, Traugott Bagge consented to serve as a justice of the peace and later sought and won a seat in the North Carolina General Assembly. Bagge's new role met with considerable favor among community leaders, who had already concluded that it would be helpful to have their own spokesman in the legislature, and who advised the residents of Salem and the other congregation towns to vote for him in a bloc.

But in most matters the leadership clung to the old ways with a crablike tenacity. In the fall of 1780 the *Land Arbeiter Conferenz*, the board charged with supervision of the "country" congregations, had issued this warning:

Members are beginning to feel the spirit of freedom in the land, and to think that as soon as the children attain their majority they are at liberty to do as they please, and no longer give their parents respect or obedience. The true idea, in conformity with the Bible and the foundation principles of the Unity, is not contrary to the law of the land, as some have supposed, for law does not abrogate the Fourth Commandment. The law does not prevent a child from being obedient to a parent, but only prevents a father from refusing to let a child set up a separate household because he thinks it would be to his advantage to keep the child at home. According to English law a child is obligated to respect his parents, and to care for them in their old age.[9]

The *Conferenz* also lamented the decline in family devotions and urged "parents in our country congregations . . . to have morning and evening prayers in their homes."

Even more alarming was the postwar rebellion against the old dress codes. The more conservative Brethren still appeared in serviceable dark jackets and knee breeches, and the Sisters in loose ankle-length dresses, their hair drawn up tight under close-fitting knit or linen caps. But many of the younger communicants had begun strutting about the streets in all sorts of outlandish garb. From the reaction of their elders, one might have thought the town had been invaded by a host of Byzantine voluptuaries. A decade after the war, Brother Franz Stauber was still able to create quite a scandal when he appeared in public "wearing a coat with shining buttons."[10] The Brethren also condemned such things as "big shaggy hats" and "hats with drooping brims, down which hang cords, or a pretty ribbon, or an unusual buckle."[11]

The same was true of black velvet breeches and "fine white cotton stockings and shammy shoes." Colors fell under the ban "when they are chosen to strike the eye, or when they are variegated; or when clothing is adorned with silver or gilt . . . and when coat and vest and breeches each has a conspicuous color." And what of Brethren who wore plain waistcoats into the meeting hall and then ostentatiously flung them open to reveal a "fine pleated shirt" or matching rows of silver buttons?[12]

And there was more: "Scarlet waistcoats . . . big buttons; and boots on which the tops are made to hang far down." Even the Sisters had grown more venturesome in this respect, and had to be warned against the evils of wearing high heels "and ornamenting the sleeves with ribbons."[13]

In their campaign to stamp out unwelcome clothing styles the Salem boards periodically sought the help of the master tailors. The *Aufseher Collegium* did so in 1793 while reprimanding residents who want "to follow each new fashion, for example, high hats with narrow brims, under-waistcoats, without tails, with two rows of white buttons and the like. It is but right that our tailors and hatmakers should not encourage this."[14]

Even as early as 1782 the town Elders had noticed that "some of the Brethren have adopted a new form of dress which is not suitable." The problem, they felt, should be discussed in open forum "and the thought brought out that not even in dress are we to be conformable to the world."[15]

But the world kept pushing in on them. By the turn of the century even that most venerable of all Moravian customs, the rule of the lot, was under severe attack. The outcry was most serious in connection with the continued use of the lot as an arbiter of marital arrangements. In 1789 an international church synod had eased the rules with respect to the "country congregations." This meant, among other things, that the town congregations (in Wachovia there were only two, Salem and Bethabara) would inevitably have to fall in line. But it would not happen all in a day. It was not until 1809 that Johanna Sophia Schober, daughter of Salem's colorful and controversial Gottlieb Schober, defied the lot and more or less got away with it; and even then she and her betrothed, Van Nemen Zevely, were forced to leave town and live as *auswärtige*, "outside" members of the congregation.

Johanna's father was himself the premier example of this post-Revolutionary mood, having at one time been held up almost as a symbol of the new and infectious "spirit of freedom" afflicting the land. In the spring of 1785 young Schober and Gottlob Krause, another controversial character, had gotten into such a violent fistfight atop a construction scaffold that the authorities accused them of severely damaging the Moravians' reputation "as a people of God," especially as they "had beaten each other in presence of all the strange people around." The Salem Elders detected in these men and certain others "a disposition . . . to set up the American spirit of freedom" in the town. "It was thought well," said the Elders, "to have an open discussion about this in Cong. Council to get to the bottom of it and to seek to do away with such a harmful tendency."[16]

Schober, tinsmith, schoolteacher, housepainter, preacher, tailor, politician, and furtive trader, was never completely to abandon his errant ways. The minutes of the *Aufseher Collegium* are filled with reports of his peccadilloes; for more than a decade there was a running argument between him and the *Collegium* regarding the whole matter. Schober could legally sell tin because he had been trained as a tinsmith and had been formally set up in the business. But he could not legally sell tallow, linen, pins, buttons, or any of the countless other articles he kept on hand from time to time. Nor could he serve as a commission agent for would-be purchasers, as he was often accused of doing. At one point the *Collegium* learned that he had been intercepting country people headed into town with their wares and offering them a higher price than they could get at the store. The obvious effect of this was to force Brother Bagge to raise his own prices. The *Collegium* admitted that Schober "knows to start his things off so well that we cannot catch him" and later added that "every time he takes new wares he has a new and special excuse for it." Finally the *Collegium* faced the issue squarely; no longer would they get into "long discussions with him about the matter and prove it all through single facts, since it is publicly known that he is trading." Rather, they would demand from him "a final declaration, whether he is now going to stop immediately this buying and selling." They got a declaration of sorts, but as can easily be guessed, it did not prove very final.[17]

For all of his personal financial ventures, which included speculations in land and ownership of a paper mill, he remained an engaging sort of fellow whose status in the community continually improved no matter how much was reported against him. Like Bagge, he had made himself too useful to be ignored. For some years he had been studying law and was to win much attention for his prosecution of the

Wilkes County land suit, the legal dispute that had caused the Moravians so much trouble during the Revolutionary years. He had even been appointed to the *Collegium*. Though later ejected for an unseemly display of temper, he never really fell out of favor. And so it went on up until the turn of the century, when he was put forward as a candidate for justice of the peace. (He later was to serve with distinction both in this office and as a state senator.) The *Collegium* approved the idea, but with certain misgivings: "We discussed how easy it can happen that a Brother thus appointed does not agree to the Community Orders entirely, so that nothing but disorder finally derives from his action. This has happened in some of our communities in Pennsylvania."[18]

The turn of the century also marked the passing of Traugott Bagge. The old man, widowed now, had remained active almost to the end of his seventy-one years, traveling widely for the community store, and sometimes for himself as well, and finally succumbing to an infectious chest condition in the early hours of April Fools' Day, 1800.

Two years later Wachovia mourned the death of Frederic William Marshall, the last of the three men who had guided the Brethren through some of its most perilous years. Bishop John Michael Graff, the spiritual leader of the Moravian congregations, had died in August of 1782, more than a year before the final signing of the peace treaty. All were men of unfailing religious conviction; all possessed a certain fortitude and sense of mission which could perhaps have seen them through even worse travail than the American Revolution. All were, in addition, an intensely practical lot for whom the adage, "The Lord helps those who help themselves," must have had a special meaning. In Bagge's case there was also a streak of contrariness which forever rules him out as a candidate for sainthood, but which, some might say, blended as a needed alloy with the more unsullied aspects of his character. Notwithstanding his brooding and often excitable temperament he had continued as Salem's official town host, or *Fremden Diener*, until his death, and was succeeded, oddly enough, by the equally temperamental Gottlieb Schober, who had once served under Bagge in the community store. The frequent clashes between the merchant and his young apprentice were both predictable and insoluble.

Bagge was one of four Brethren hauled into court soon after the war and charged with depreciating the paper currency. Similar charges against the tanner Herbst and the potter Aust, who was probably the guiltiest of the lot, were dismissed because of technical deficiencies in the arraignment. Bagge's trial lasted for four hours, with many of the courthouse hangers-on voluntarily testifying in his behalf. So much was said about the defendants and their "real value to the State" that the ones standing around watching the proceedings "expected nothing other than that he would be released as cleared."[19] But he was found guilty and fined fifty pounds.

Despite this lone brush with the law, which seems to have been taken seriously by no one except the judge who assessed the fine, and despite his failure to get elected to a second legislative term, Bagge had developed close and enduring relationships with many of the state's political leaders, from Governor Martin on down, winning new respect for his scrupulousness, his intelligence and sound judgment, and even his tact—an attribute which, as we have seen, was to win him no fame in his own community.

The case against Bagge was summed up by one of his assistants, John Chitty, who in late 1789 had gone running to the Elders Conference with what by now was an all-too-familiar complaint: "John Chitty represents that he can no longer work in harmony with Br. Bagge in the store, says he can do nothing any more to suit Bagge." Attempts at reconciliation proved futile, and Chitty was eventually left to go his own way. But, said the Elders, "it was thought best not to speak with Br. Bagge about it unless he brings it up."[20]

Bagge's penchant for detail and the exactitude with which he conducted his affairs—and expected others to conduct theirs—were qualities deemed more admirable from a distance perhaps than at close range. But they were also the qualities which made him the fussiest of record keepers in a town renowned for its string-saving ways, and which consequently have made his chronicles[21] of the Revolutionary years such a valuable resource for historians. They were the same qualities, furthermore, which worked so effectively for the Moravians when he was defending their legal position against voracious liberty men and vindictive politicians. The esteem in which he was held seemed only to increase as the years went by. Shortly after his death an obituary celebrating his achievements appeared in a Philadelphia newspaper. About the same time former Governor Martin, who could boast of certain literary pretensions, sent a "poem" which, as he told Brother Marshall in a letter, "flowed from my Pen spontaneously":

What stroke of Fate has Salem's Son befell
Their silent Griefs some sad Disaster tell
No common Loss their heaving Sighs deplore
Bagge alas the Friend of Man's no more
True to his Trusts who ever firmly stood
A bright Example! honest–wise–and good–
From *Suecia's*[22] Realms in early Youth he came
Led by Religion's pure and sacred Flame
Lusatia's[23] Brethren claim'd him as their own
Mong whom his Virtues long have brightly shone;
There not confin'd but to the World around
Defur'd to Man a gen'ral Good redound
Columbia's Sons his generous Worth detail
With sympathetic Tears his Fate bewail.

So gentle Spirit to those Realms above
Where Peace & Friendship reign with holy Love
Thy much lov'd *Zinzendorff* will joyfull rise
Thy *Spangenberg*, & greet thee to the Skies
Thy *Watteville*, & all th' united Choir
Will glow to meet thee with a sacred Fire:
With tenfold Talents gain'd, go meet thy Lord!
Enjoy the welcome Promise of his Word! ! ![24]

It remains only to be said that the Revolution was in many ways an even more momentous affair in the lives of these Moravians, who had sought to have nothing to do with it, than in the lives of the American people as a whole. It could hardly have been otherwise. Though an authoritarian people—"we believe with all our heart that where there is any authority, it is of God"[25]—they could not remain forever aloof from the democratic ideals which they in a larger sense shared. They had themselves become an instrument of democracy in this wild new democratic land. By insisting on their right not to bear arms or swear public oaths, or even to affirm oaths which conflicted with their sense of right and wrong, they had laid claim to the most thoroughly democratic idea of all—the right of dissent—and had done so without forfeiting either their property or the respect of the more responsible revolutionary leaders. With the Moravian Brethren this right of dissent, this belief that man's conscience is larger than man's wars, was already an ancient tradition more than half a century before Henry David Thoreau published his famous pamphlet on civil disobedience (though disobedience was a word, a concept, that the Brethren would have rejected absolutely) and almost two hundred years before these ideas had become in any way acceptable to large segments of the American public.

There can be no doubt that the Revolution greatly altered the habits and enlarged the perspective of this pious, inward-looking, self-sufficient and somewhat austere people. But is it not also possible that they in their own small way altered the conduct of the Revolution? Or if that is too large a claim, it is at least true that they forced many of their political leaders to ponder deeply the ultimate meaning of this war, and in the end perhaps to understand its central paradox: to understand, in other words, that the democratic ideas for which they had fought so violently and so stubbornly belonged also to those who had refused, even at considerable risk to themselves, to take any part in the struggle, who had sought only to remain "peaceful and undisturbed as the quiet people of the land."[26]

Revolutionary Calendar

1771

16 May — Governor William Tryon and North Carolina militia smash Regulator rebellion at prerevolutionary Battle of Alamance.

1774

5 September — First Continental Congress, meeting at Philadelphia, adopts economic sanctions against Great Britain and advises the colonists to arm themselves.

1775

19 April — Patriots and British regulars clash at Lexington and Concord.

10 May — A patriot force under Ethan Allen captures Fort Ticonderoga on Lake Champlain. Second Continental Congress convenes in Philadelphia.

31 May — A convention in Mecklenburg County, North Carolina, adopts a set of resolves annulling all laws and commissions deriving their authority from the king or Parliament and appoints a committee of selectmen to take over the local government.

15 June — George Washington appointed commander-in-chief of Continental forces.

17 June — British seize Bunker Hill with heavy losses.

5 and 6 July — Second Continental Congress reaffirms its attachment to the king and at the same time adopts a "Declaration of the Causes and Necessities of Taking Up Arms."

11 December	At Great Bridge, Virginia, a patriot force from North Carolina assists Virginians in the rout of a loyalist army recruited by Governor Dunmore of that province.

1776

15 January	Thomas Paine publishes *Common Sense*, a pamphlet destined to convert thousands to the cause of independence.
27 February	North Carolina Patriots rout loyalist forces at Moores Creek Bridge, preventing an intended junction with the British and temporarily saving their province from invasion.
17 March	Under the threat of siege guns, the British evacuate Boston.
4 July	Congress votes unanimously for independence.
15 September	British occupy New York City, barely failing to cut off the retreat of Washington's army.
28 October	Battle of White Plains. Lord Howe moves against Washington, captures key hill position, suffering more than 300 casualties and inflicting about 200.
18 November	Washington, accompanied by a force under General Nathanael Greene, begins retreat across New Jersey, pursued by Lord Charles Cornwallis, later crossing the Delaware River into Pennsylvania.
26 December	Washington, recrossing the Delaware, surprises Hessian garrison at Trenton and scores major victory.

1777

3 January	Washington drives the British out of Princeton, New Jersey, and retires to winter quarters in Morristown.
28 February	In England, General John Burgoyne unveils plans for a three-pronged attack which he believes will isolate New England.
11 September	Lord Howe attacks Washington at Brandywine Creek, driving the American army back toward Philadelphia.
4 October	Americans driven from Germantown, Pennsylvania.
17 October	General Burgoyne surrenders his 5,700-man army after the collapse of his five-month campaign against New England.
17 December	Lord North's government prepares a new plan of reconciliation only to find Americans solid for independence.

1778

6 February	France enters war on the side of the Americans.
28 June	With the horrors of the Valley Forge winter behind them, Washington's forces engage the British at Monmouth Courthouse. The British, now under the command of Sir Henry Clinton, retreat to New York.
29 December	British take Savannah in what Clinton hopes is the first step toward the reduction of the American South.

1779

21 June	Spain enters war against Britain while at the same time refusing to recognize American independence.
14 August	After seven months of steady fighting, with neither side able to gain the upper hand, the United States concludes a proposed peace pact. Among the major demands: independence, complete British evacuation of American territory, and the right to free navigation of the Mississippi.
23 September	In the war's most famous sea battle, John Paul Jones, commanding the *Bonhomme Richard*, captures the British *Serapis* after a devastating engagement which had seemed certain to end in his defeat.
9 October	A protracted French siege of Savannah is drawn off in failure.

1780

5 June	With both Georgia and the city of Charleston, South Carolina, now in loyalist hands, Clinton departs for New York, leaving Lord Cornwallis to take charge of the war in the South.
9 July	Russia persuades European neutrals to join with her in a League of Armed Neutrality, thus disrupting Britain's blockade efforts against France and Spain.
16 August	British strengthen hold on South Carolina by crushing American forces at Camden.
21 September	Benedict Arnold, under fire for his performance as American military commander in Philadelphia, contacts the enemy and begins negotiations which will end with his betrayal of the American cause.
7 October	Americans stall British advance in the South with stunning victory at Kings Mountain.
14 October	General Greene takes charge of the southern armies.

1781

17 January	At Cowpens, in the South Carolina foothills, a retreating American force under Brigadier Daniel Morgan chops the British to pieces.
15 March	Ending a two-month pursuit of General Greene, Cornwallis attacks the Americans in a savage battle at Guilford Courthouse, the British gaining the field but with such huge losses that the advantage lies all the other way.
8 September	After repeatedly turning defeat into victory, Guilford Courthouse style, Greene attacks the British at Eutaw Springs, South Carolina, again with mixed results. By fall only Charleston and its immediate vicinity remain in British control.
19 October	Cornwallis surrenders at Yorktown.

1782

20 March	Lord North's ministry falls and Britain decides to sue for peace.
30 November	Belligerents sign preliminary articles of peace.

1783

20 January	The articles take effect after Britain's settlement with France.

Notes

Chapter 1

1. Lorenz Bagge to Ettwein, 9 May 1768, Moravian Archives, Pa.
2. Memoir of Traugott Bagge, Moravian Archives, Winston-Salem, N.C.
3. Ibid.
4. The business manager and treasurer of a congregation or choir.
5. After the German *Wachau*, the name of an Austrian estate that had once belonged to the Zinzendorf family. The 100,000-acre Wachovia tract included all of present-day Winston-Salem and much of its suburban area.
6. Jethro Rumple, *A History of Rowan County, North Carolina*, p. 89.
7. Adelaide L. Fries, ed., *Records of the Moravians in North Carolina*, 2:651–52.
8. Worship services in song. A *Singstunde* consists of hymns arranged so as to develop a specific devotional theme and designed to take the place of a sermon.
9. Charles Woodmason, *The Carolina Backcountry on the Eve of the Revolution*, p. 77.
10. Fries, *Records of the Moravians*, 1:49.
11. John Lawson, *Lawson's History of North Carolina*, p. 43.
12. Fries, *Records of the Moravians*, 1:59.
13. Bethabara and Bethania.
14. Woodmason, *Carolina Backcountry*, pp. 77–78.
15. Woodmason's derogatory phrase need not be taken as representative of all the frontier settlers. He was speaking, of course, of the Scottish Presbyterians, known as Scotch-Irish because their forebears had settled in Ulster (northern Ireland). They were by far the most numerous of the groups that poured into western North Carolina in the middle of the eighteenth century. But it should also be remembered that there were a great many German settlers other than Moravians in the area, and in addition a sizable body of Englishmen who had migrated west out of the coastal plain.
16. Fries, *Records of the Moravians*, 2:816, 682–83, 761.
17. Tryon to Shelburne, quoted in Hugh Talmage Lefler and Albert Ray Newsome, *North Carolina*, p. 173.
18. Carl Bridenbaugh, *Myths and Realities: Societies of the Colonial South*, p. 161.
19. William S. Powell, Thomas J. Farnham, and James K. Huhta, eds. and comps., *The Regulators in North Carolina*, p. 251.
20. A man designated as a "servant of strangers," appointed to attend to the needs of visitors, introduce them to the town, and acquaint them with Moravian customs.
21. Fries, *Records of the Moravians*, 1:452.
22. Ibid.
23. Powell, Farnham, and Huhta, *The Regulators*, prefatory notes.
24. Fries, *Records of the Moravians*, 1:457. Husbands, or whoever it was, apparently was looking for help for the Regulator wounded, but according to the Bethabara diary Dr. Bonn "excused himself, as there were patients in the neighborhood who needed him."

25. Ibid., p. 458.

26. Tryon on the Battle of Alamance, quoted in Lefler and Newsome, *North Carolina*, p. 176.

27. Fries, *Records of the Moravians*, 1:338.

28. Ibid., p. 340.

29. Ibid., pp. 354, 355, 339.

30. Ibid., pp. 463, 466.

31. Ibid., pp. 464, 465.

32. Ibid., p. 467.

Chapter 2

1. Adelaide L. Fries, ed., *Records of the Moravians in North Carolina*, 1:314.

2. Ibid., p. 324.

3. Ibid., pp. 320, 322.

4. Ibid., 2:618.

5. Ibid., 1:391.

6. John F. Bivins, Jr., "The Development of the Trades in Wachovia," p. 6.

7. Fries, *Records of the Moravians*, 1:110.

8. *The North Carolina Journal*, Halifax, N.C., 20 February 1793. A reprint appeared in the *Old Salem Gleaner*, Summer-Fall issue, 1972.

9. The business organization of a congregation or choir, or of the church as a whole.

10. Fries, *Records of the Moravians*, 2:883.

Chapter 3

1. Adelaide L. Fries, ed., *Records of the Moravians in North Carolina*, 2:874, 888.

2. Ibid., pp. 876, 852.

3. Ibid., pp. 848, 888.

4. Ibid., p. 848.

5. Ibid., pp. 882, 850.

6. Ibid., 3:1070.

7. Kenneth Gardiner Hamilton, *John Ettwein and the Moravian Church during the Revolutionary Period*, p. 132.

8. Ibid.

9. Ibid., p. 137.

10. Ibid., p. 140.

11. Fries, *Records of the Moravians*, 2:840.

12. Ibid., 1:66.

13. Ibid., 2:840–41.

14. J. Taylor Hamilton and Kenneth G. Hamilton, *History of the Moravian Church*, p. 136.

15. J. Taylor Hamilton, *The Recognition of the Unitas Fratrum as an Old Episcopal Church by the Parliament of Great Britain in 1749*, p. 46.

16. John Henry Clewell, *History of Wachovia in North Carolina*, p. 137.

17. Fries, *Records of the Moravians*, 2:887.

18. Ibid.

19. Ibid., p. 898.

20. Ibid., 3:1053.

Chapter 4

1. Adelaide L. Fries, *Records of the Moravians in North Carolina*, 2:904.

2. Ibid., p. 907.

3. William L. Saunders, ed., *The Colonial Records of North Carolina*, 9:1194, 1191.

4. Fries, *Records of the Moravians*, 3:1026.

5. Ibid.

6. Williams to Caswell, 23 July 1777, Richard Caswell Papers, Duke University Library, Durham, N.C.

7. Fries, *Records of the Moravians*, 3:1027.

8. Memoir of Traugott Bagge, Moravian Archives, Winston-Salem, N.C.

9. Fries, *Records of the Moravians*, 3:1028, 2:907.

10. Ibid., 3:1348.

11. Ibid., p. 1240.

12. Ibid., 1:457.

13. Ibid., 3:1028.

14. Congregation house. In most early Moravian settlements the *Gemein Haus* contained a large meeting hall for worship services along with living quarters for church officials and visitors.

15. Fries, *Records of the Moravians*, 3:1066, 1067, 1036, 1118.

16. Ibid., p. 1036.

17. Ibid., p. 1067.

18. Ibid., pp. 1031–32.

Chapter 5

1. Adelaide L. Fries, ed., *Records of the Moravians in North Carolina*, 3:1072.

2. Ibid., p. 1073.

3. Ibid.

4. Ibid., p. 1100.

5. Ibid., p. 1073.

6. Ibid., pp. 1232, 1139.

7. Ibid., pp. 1138, 1139.

8. Ibid., p. 1129.

9. Erika Huber, trans. Minutes of the Aufseher Collegium, 6 February 1777, Moravian Archives, Winston-Salem, N.C.

10. Fries, *Records of the Moravians*, 3:1164.

11. Ibid., pp. 1166, 1167.

12. Ibid., p. 1144.

13. Ibid., p. 1206.

14. Ibid., p. 1241.

15. Ibid., p. 1205.

16. Ibid., p. 1209.

17. Huber, Aufseher Collegium Minutes, 3 May 1775, Moravian Archives, Winston-Salem, N.C.

18. Edmund Schwarze, trans., Minutes of the Elders Conference, 13 May 1775, Moravian Archives, Winston-Salem, N.C.

19. Ibid., 21 July 1778.

20. Fries, *Records of the Moravians*, 3:1377.

21. Ibid., p. 1366.

22. Ibid., p. 1377.

23. Ibid., p. 1378.

24. John Henry Clewell, *History of Wachovia in North Carolina*, p. 144.

25. Fries, *Records of the Moravians*, 3:1130.

26. Ibid., pp. 1379, 1380.

27. Ibid., 1:469; 3:1381.

28. Ibid., p. 1381.

29. Ibid., pp. 1381, 1377, 1381.

30. Ibid., pp. 1383, 1207.

31. Ibid., p. 1385.
32. Ibid., pp. 1263, 1287.
33. Ibid., p. 1254.
34. Ibid., p. 1290.

Chapter 6

1. Adelaide L. Fries, ed., *Records of the Moravians in North Carolina*, 3:1225.
2. Ibid., p. 1226.
3. Erika Huber, trans. Minutes of the Aufseher Collegium, 25 March 1779, Moravian Archives, Winston-Salem, N.C.
4. Fries, *Records of the Moravians*, 3:1218.
5. Huber, Aufseher Collegium Minutes, 28 August 1780, Moravian Archives, Winston-Salem, N.C.
6. Ibid., 22 January 1777, 24 November 1779.
7. Ibid., 8 January 1777, 4 April 1780.
8. Fries, *Records of the Moravians*, 3:1326.
9. Huber, Aufseher Collegium Minutes, 2 December 1783, Moravian Archives, Winston-Salem, N.C.
10. Fries, *Records of the Moravians*, 3:1030.
11. Huber, Aufseher Collegium Minutes, 5 May 1779, Moravian Archives, Winston-Salem, N.C.
12. Fries, *Records of the Moravians*, 3:1326.
13. Ibid.
14. Ibid., p. 1296.

Chapter 7

1. Adelaide L. Fries, ed., *Records of the Moravians in North Carolina*, 3:1277–78.
2. Ibid.
3. Ibid., p. 1112.
4. Ibid., p. 1283.
5. Ibid.
6. Ibid., p. 1308.
7. Ibid., pp. 1316, 1250, 1227.
8. Banastre Tarleton, *A History of the Campaigns of 1780 and 1781 in the Southern Provinces of North America*, p. 160.
9. Fries, *Records of the Moravians*, 4:1902.
10. Ibid., p. 1626.
11. Ibid., p. 1565.
12. Ibid., p. 1553.
13. Ibid., p. 1563.
14. Ibid., p. 1572.
15. Ibid., p. 1560.
16. Ibid., pp. 1542, 1551.
17. John H. Wheeler, *Historical Sketches of North Carolina*, p. 385.
18. E. W. Caruthers, *Interesting Revolutionary Incidents and Sketches of Character*, p. 263.
19. Fries, *Records of the Moravians*, 4:1642.
20. Ibid., p. 1561.
21. Ibid., p. 1607.
22. Ibid., p. 1644.
23. Ibid., p. 1571.
24. Ibid., p. 1644.

25. Ibid.

26. Sumner to Gates, Walter Clark, ed., *State Records of North Carolina, 1777–1790*, 14:692.

27. Fries, *Records of the Moravians*, 4:1571–72.

28. Smallwood to Gates, in Clark, *State Records*, 14:699.

29. Martin to Fries, unpublished correspondence, Moravian Archives, Winston-Salem, N.C.

30. Fries, *Records of the Moravians*, 4:1907.

31. Ibid., p. 1632.

Chapter 8

1. Greene to Morgan, quoted in Phillips Russell, *North Carolina in the Revolutionary War*, p. 220.

2. William A. Graham, *General Joseph Graham and His Papers on North Carolina Revolutionary History*, p. 310.

3. Bethania had come to be known as Hoozertown after the great number of Hausers who had settled there, and was still known by that name well into the present century.

4. E. W. Caruthers, *Interesting Revolutionary Incidents and Sketches*, p. 33.

5. Ibid., p. 34.

6. Ibid., pp. 34–35.

7. Adelaide L. Fries, ed., *Records of the Moravians in North Carolina*, 4:1766.

8. Ibid., p. 1742.

9. Caruthers, *Revolutionary Incidents*, p. 36.

10. Fries, *Records of the Moravians*, 4:1674.

11. Under a 1789 act that was part of a package of laws setting up the university.

12. Fries, *Records of the Moravians*, 4:1674.

13. Ibid., p. 1675.

14. Ibid., p. 1775.

15. Ibid., pp. 1907–8

16. Ibid., p. 1908.

17. Ibid., p. 1675.

18. This apartment had been built as part of the community store.

19. Fries, *Records of the Moravians*, 4:1780.

20. Ibid., pp. 1676, 1677.

21. Ibid.

22. Ibid., pp. 1678–79.

23. Graham, *General Joseph Graham*, p. 312.

24. Fries, *Records of the Moravians*, 4:1679.

25. Ibid., p. 1681.

26. Ibid., pp. 1682–83.

27. Ibid., p. 1684.

28. Ibid.

29. Ibid., p. 1687.

30. Ibid., p. 1688.

31. Erika Huber, trans., Aufseher Collegium Minutes, 22 May 1783, Moravian Archives, Winston-Salem, N.C.

32. Fries, *Records of the Moravians*, 4:1711, 1880.

33. Ettwein to Marshall, late 1765, Moravian Archives, Bethlehem, Pa.

34. Fries, *Records of the Moravians*, 4:1656.

35. Sir Henry Clinton, *The American Rebellion*, p. 510.

36. Fries, *Records of the Moravians*, 4:1756.

37. Ibid., pp. 1734, 1735.

38. A hall where worship services were held. The *Saal* was originally part of the *Gemein Haus*, but later on many separate edifices built for worship were known by this name.

39. Fries, *Records of the Moravians*, 4:1705.

40. Ibid., p. 1788.

41. Ibid., p. 1914.

42. Ibid.

Chapter 9

1. Adelaide L. Fries, ed., *Records of the Moravians in North Carolina*, 4:1839.

2. Ibid., pp. 1919–20.

3. Ibid., p. 1841.

4. Ibid., p. 1921.

5. Ibid.

6. Erika Huber, trans., Minutes of the Aufseher Collegium, 10 July 1783, Moravian Archives, Winston-Salem, N.C.

7. Alonzo Thomas Dill, *Governor Tryon and His Palace*, p. 211.

8. There had never been an outright prohibition against public service. Dr. Jacob Bonn, the saddler Charles Holder, the Bethania weaver and farmer Michael Hauser—these and other members of the Unity had served at one time or another as justices of the peace.

9. Fries, *Records of the Moravians*, 4:1609.

10. Huber, Aufseher Collegium Minutes, 7 February 1792, Moravian Archives, Winston-Salem, N.C.

11. Fries, *Records of the Moravians*, 5:2177.

12. Ibid., pp. 2177–78.

13. Ibid., p. 2178.

14. Ibid., 6:2484.

15. Edmund Schwarze, trans., Minutes of the Elders Conference, 17 April 1782, Moravian Archives, Winston-Salem, N.C.

16. Schwarze, Elders Conference Minutes, 29 June 1785; Huber, Aufseher Collegium Minutes, 29 June 1785; Schwarze, Elders Conference Minutes, 6 July 1785, Moravian Archives, Winston-Salem, N.C.

17. Huber, Aufseher Collegium Minutes, 15 July 1788, 7 July 1789, 17 July 1789, Moravian Archives, Winston-Salem, N.C.

18. Ibid., 16 November 1802.

19. Fries, *Records of the Moravians*, 5:2074.

20. Schwarze, Elders Conference Minutes, 2 December 1789, Moravian Archives, Winston-Salem, N.C.

21. Bagge's account, printed as part of the Moravian Records, extends only through the year 1779.

22. A reference to Bagge's Swedish origin.

23. Upper Lusatia in Saxony, where Herrnhut, the Moravians' international church center, had been built.

24. Moravian Archives, Winston-Salem, N.C.

25. Kenneth Gardiner Hamilton, *John Ettwein and the Moravian Church During the Revolutionary Period*, p. 159.

26. Fries, *Records of the Moravians*, 1:322.

Bibliography

Ahlstrom, Sydney E. *A Religious History of the American People*. New Haven: Yale University Press, 1972.

Anscombe, Francis C. *I Have Called You Friends: The Story of Quakerism in North Carolina*. Boston: Christopher Publishing House, 1959.

Bailey, J. D. *Commanders at King's Mountain*. Gaffney, S.C.: Ed. H. De Camp, 1926.

Bivins, John F., Jr. "The Development of the Trades in Wachovia." Research paper, Department of Education and Interpretation, Old Salem, Inc., 1969.

Brawley, James S. *The Rowan Story, 1753–1953: A Narrative History of Rowan County, North Carolina*. Salisbury: Rowan Printing Co., 1953.

Bridenbaugh, Carl. *Myths and Realities: Societies of the Colonial South*. 1952. Reprint. New York: Atheneum, 1965.

Caruthers, E. W. *Interesting Revolutionary Incidents and Sketches of Character, Chiefly in the Old North State*, second series. Philadelphia: Hayes and Zell, 1856.

Clark, Walter, ed. *State Records of North Carolina, 1777–1790*. 16 vols. Winston-Salem and Goldsboro, 1895–1905.

Clinton, Sir Henry. *The American Rebellion*. Edited by William B. Willcox. New Haven: Yale University Press, 1954.

Clewell, John Henry. *History of Wachovia in North Carolina*. New York: Doubleday, Page and Co., 1902.

Davis, Burke. *The Cowpens–Guilford Courthouse Campaign*. Philadelphia: J. B. Lippincott Co., 1962.

De Schweinitz, Edmund. *History of the Unitas Fratrum*. Bethlehem: The Moravian Publication Concern, 1901.

Dill, Alonzo Thomas. *Governor Tryon and His Palace*. Chapel Hill: University of North Carolina Press, 1955.

Fries, Adelaide L., ed. *Records of the Moravians in North Carolina.* 7 vols. 1922–43. Reprint. Raleigh: State Department of Archives and History, 1968 and 1970.

Graham, William A. *General Joseph Graham and His Papers on North Carolina Revolutionary History.* Raleigh: William A. Graham, 1904.

Hamilton, J. Taylor. *The Recognition of the Unitas Fratrum as an Old Episcopal Church by the Parliament of Great Britain in 1749.* Monograph. Transactions of the Moravian Historical Society, vol. 2, part 2. Bethlehem: Times Publishing Co., 1925.

Hamilton, J. Taylor, and Hamilton, Kenneth G. *History of the Moravian Church: The Renewed Unitas Fratrum, 1722–1957.* Bethlehem and Winston-Salem: Interprovincial Board of Christian Education, Moravian Church in America, 1967.

Hamilton, Kenneth G. *John Ettwein and the Moravian Church During the Revolutionary Period.* Bethlehem: Times Publishing Co., 1940.

Hickerson, Thomas Felix. *Happy Valley: History and Genealogy.* Durham: Thomas Felix Hickerson, 1940.

Lawson, John. *Lawson's History of North Carolina.* 1714. Reprint. Richmond: Garrett and Massie, 1961.

Lazenby, Mary Elinor, comp. *Catawba Frontier.* Washington: Mary Elinor Lazenby, 1950.

Lefler, Hugh Talmage, and Newsome, Albert Ray. *North Carolina: The History of a Southern State.* Chapel Hill: University of North Carolina Press, 1954.

Lefler, Hugh Talmage and Powell, William S. *Colonial North Carolina.* New York: Charles Scribner's Sons, 1973.

Morison, Samuel Eliot. *The Oxford History of the American People.* New York: Oxford University Press, 1965.

Powell, William S.; Farnham, Thomas J.; and Huhta, James K., eds. *The Regulators in North Carolina: A Documentary History, 1759–1776.* Raleigh: State Department of Archives and History, 1971.

Ramsey, Robert W. *Carolina Cradle: Settlement of the Northwest Carolina Frontier, 1747–1762.* Chapel Hill: University of North Carolina Press, 1964.

Rankin, Hugh R. *The North Carolina Continentals.* Chapel Hill: University of North Carolina Press, 1971.

Riggsbee, Belinda. "The North Carolina Moravians During the American Revolution." Seminar paper, University of North Carolina at Greensboro, 1974.

Rumple, Jethro. *A History of Rowan County, North Carolina.* 1881. Reprint. Salisbury: The Elizabeth Steele Chapter, Daughters of the American Revolution, 1929.

Russell, Phillips. *North Carolina in the Revolutionary War.* Charlotte: Heritage Printers, 1965.

Saunders, William L., ed. *The Colonial Records of North Carolina, 1662–1776*. 10 vols. Raleigh, 1886–90.

Tarleton, Banastre. *A History of the Campaigns of 1780 and 1781 in the Southern Provinces of North America*. 1787. Reprint. New York: New York Times and Arno Press, 1968.

Wall, James W. *History of Davie County*. Mocksville: Davie County Historical Publishing Association, 1969.

Wheeler, John H. *Historical Sketches of North Carolina*. 1851. Reprint. New York: Frederick H. Hitchcock, 1925.

Woodmason, Charles. *The Carolina Backcountry on the Eve of the Revolution: The Journal and Other Writings of Charles Woodmason, Anglican Itinerant*. Edited by Richard J. Hooker. Chapel Hill: University of North Carolina Press, 1953.

Index

Cornwallis, 108; menaced by North Carolina militiamen, 111–12; gains protection of Captain Joseph Graham, 111–12; discourages legislative meeting in Salem, 120; appointed as justice of the peace and elected to legislature, 127; death of, 131; convicted on charges of depreciating paper currency, 132; as friend of Governor Alexander Martin, 132; at odds with John Chitty, 132; eulogized in Philadelphia newspaper and in a verse written by Governor Martin, 133

Baptists, 7, 11–12
Battle Creek, 92, 93
Baumgarten, Marie, 85
Beatty's Ford, 96
Bethabara, 3, 5, 23, 36, 51, 81, 89; described by Charles Woodmason, 8–9; founding and settlement of, 8–13 passim; visited by Governor William Tryon, 17, 20–22; prosperity of, 24; beginnings of trade in, 28; tavern at, 49; disturbances in, 83–84; Tory hunt at, 84, 89, 114; British soldiers and Tories imprisoned at, 93–94; British army in, 101, 103; occupied by Colonel John Preston's troops, 113
Bethania, 5; founding of, 24; Revolutionary sentiment of, 59, 100–101; visited by wives of Tory fugitives, 88; appearance of Tories in, 89–91; occupied by British army, 100–103; views of British toward, 100–101; as "Hoozertown," 101
Bibighaus, George, 77, 107
Blum, Jacob, rejects appointment to Surry County Committee of Safety, 34; to Hillsborough with Traugott Bagge, 64; takes affirmation renouncing king, 71
Bonn, Dr. Jacob: meets with Regulators, 15; visited by Regulator's leader, 17; rejects appointment to Surry County Committee of Safety and stripped of authority as justice of peace, 34; robbed by British, 110; provides medical aid for wounded Americans, 117; criticized by John Ettwein, 117; death of, 118
Boone, Daniel, 82
Booner, Joseph, 85
Bridenbaugh, Carl: quoted, 13–14
British army. See Cornwallis, Lord Charles
Broadbay, Maine, 110
Brunswick, 20
Bryan, Morgan, 83
Bryan, Samuel: raises Tory army and

marches against Whigs, 83; fights with Richmond Pearson, 87
Bunker Hill, 32
Burke, Edmund, 116
Butler, William, 14

C
Calvin, John, 10, 11
Calvinist doctrines, 10–11
Camden: battle of, 83, 86
Campbell, Colonel William: as leader of Bethabara Tory hunt, 84; seeks supplies, 85; provides help for Moravians, 114–15
Carteret, Lord (Earl Granville), 6
Caruthers, Eli W.: quoted, 93, 101, 103
Caswell, Governor Richard: as commander at Moores Creek Bridge, 48; meets with Traugott Bagge, 66
Catawba River, 96
Charles II, 79
Charleston, South Carolina: as trade center, 20, 21, 29, 77; as theater of war, 54, 81, 83
Charlotte, 83, 91
Chelcicky, Peter of, 36, 81
Cheraw, South Carolina, 95
Cherokees, 5, 105; defeated by patriot forces, 52
Chitty, John, 132
Choir system, 9
Church of England. See Anglican Church
Cloyd, Major Joseph, 92
Colonial government, 6–7
Colson's Mill: battle of, 83,89
Common housekeeping. See Moravians, common housekeeping of
Community store: in Bethabara, 3, 29; in Salem, 29, 54, 75, 77
Concord, Massachusetts: battle of, 32
Congaree River, 54
Congregation Council in Salem, 88
Congress money, 74
Constitution, state, 65; federal, 125
Continental Hospital, 117
Corbin, Francis, 16
Cornwallis, Lord Charles, 87, 91, 112; as commander of British army in the South, 81; southern campaign of, 81, 83, 88–89, 95–103, 108, 119; pursues General Nathanael Greene, 96–103; at Hillsborough, 98; proclaims restoration of royal rule and seeks help of Tories, 98, 119; at Guilford Courthouse, 98–100; crosses Shallow Ford, 98, 100; marches through Wachovia, 100–103, 108; occupies Bethania, 100–103; exac-

tions of, in Bethania, 102–3; entertained by Traugott Bagge and Frederic William Marshall, 108; occupies Friedland, 110; marches to Wilmington, 119; and views on North Carolina as battleground, 119; abandoned by Tories, 119

Country congregations. *See* Moravians, country congregations of

Cowan's Ford: battle of, 97; Pickens Militia at, 100

Cowpens, 114; battle of, 95–96

Cross Creek (Fayetteville): as trade center, 29, 41, 77; as loyalist stronghold, 43, 45, 48; visited by Christian Heckewalder, 48, 66

Cumberland Mountains, 82

Currency: Continental, 74. *See also* Moravians, currency problems of

D

Dan River, 5, 98, 114

Davidson, General William L., 96, 97

Davidson County, 50

Davie, General William R., 83

Davie County, 92

Declaration of Independence, 74; posted on Salem Tavern, 55; response of Moravians to, 55–56; news of received in Bethabara, 56

Democracy, 127; Moravian attitude toward, 37, 127–34 passim

Dixon, Joseph, 117, 118

Dryden, John: quoted, 79

Dunkards, 71

Dutchman's Creek, 87

E

Easter sunrise service: origins of, 122–23; superstitions concerning, 123

Elders Conference: in Salem, 23, 24, 30, 41, 56, 65, 129, 130, 132

English Settlement. *See* Hope

Ernst, John Jacob: as Bethania minister, 91; mediates with British, 102–3

Ettwein, John: visits Governor Tryon, 19–20; counsels Moravians with regard to war policy, 34; as exponent of pacifism, 34, 36–37; criticizes Jacob Bonn, 117

F

Fanning, Edmund, 14, 19

Farmington, 100

Ferguson, Colonel Patrick, 89

Firearms, 41, 43, 48

First Battle of Shallow Ford. *See* Shallow Ford, battle of

First Continental Congress, 33

Fockel, Gottlieb, 49

Forks of the Yadkin, 87

Forsyth County, 50

Fort Johnston, 44

Fort Moultrie: battle of, 53–54

Fourth of July: proclaimed as holiday by Governor Alexander Martin, 123; celebrated by Moravians, 124, 125

Francis, Captain, 92

Freedom of religion, 61

French and Indian War, 5, 24

Frey, George, 52–53

Friedberg, 53; as focus of enlistment activity, 51–52; disturbances in, 80–81, 105, 107; smallpox in, 117

Friedland, 108; occupied by British, 110

Fries, Dr. Adelaide, 38, 118

Fritz, John Christian, 84–85

Fulneck, England, 4

G

Gemein Haus: in Salem, 52, 122, 123, 125

Gemein Nachrichten, 4

George III, 32, 39, 55, 110; birthday of, celebrated in Bethabara, 21–22

God's Acre: in Bethabara and Salem, 123

Göteborg, Sweden, 4

Graff, John Michael: as minister and diarist in Salem, 32; criticizes Moravian war sentiment, 35; criticizes liberty men, 42; reacts to Declaration of Independence, 55–56; comments on need for prompt payment of taxes, 60; laments illegal land entries, 62; expresses relief at Moravian military exemption, 71; criticizes labor strike by Single Brethren, 72–73; comments on money problems, 74, 78; comments on smallpox epidemic and on migration to Kentucky, 82; reports on rising of Tories, 91; death of, 131

Graham, Captain Joseph: skirmishes with British, 93, 100; joins Pickens Militia, 100; assists Traugott Bagge, 111–12

Granville, Earl. *See* Carteret, Lord

Granville County: political disorders in, 13

Granville District, 6

Great Awakening, 11

Great Philadelphia Wagon Road, 7, 27–28

Great Sabbath, 122

Greene, General Nathanael, 37, 92, 104; takes command of American armies in the South, 95; retreats from Cornwallis, 96–99; at Salisbury, 97; crosses Yadkin River, 97–98; crosses Dan River, 98; at

Guilford Courthouse, 98–100; criticizes North Carolina militiamen, 98, 100; in Virginia, 98; camps at Abbotts Creek, 107; forced to deny protection for Moravians, 108

Greter, Jacob, Sr., 105

Guild system in Salem, 30

Guilford Courthouse: battle of, 98–100, 119; and effect on Moravians, 115

H

Halifax, 51, 71

Halifax County: political disorders in, 12

Hamilton, Alexander, 36

Hanging Rock: battle of, 83, 89

Hanson, Lieutenant Samuel, 113

Harris, Joseph, 15, 16

Hartman, George, 52

Harvey, John, 44

Hasell, Judge James, 19

Hauser, George, Jr., 35

Hauser, George, Sr., 34, 102

Hauser, John, 35

Hauser, Michael, 102

Haversham, Colonel Joseph, 86

Heckewalder, Christian, 65, 77; besieged by Whigs and Tories at Cross Creek, 48; at odds with Traugott Bagge, 64; as emissary to Halifax, 71

Heinzmann, Johann: attacked by army deserters, 53; in Friedland, 110

Heinzmann, Mrs. Johann (Anna Catharina), 110

Herrnhut, Germany, 38, 80; as international Moravian church center, 4, 24, 123

Hillsborough, 27; riot in, 14; as temporary seat of state government, 65–70 passim

Hillsborough Courthouse. See Hillsborough, riot in

Hill, Philipp, 35, 52

Hill, William, 44, 94, 114

Holbert, Captain, 114

Holder, Charles, 31, 107

Hoozertown. See Bethania

Hope: Moravian "English Settlement," 84–85

Howe, General Sir William, 61

Howell, Rednap, 13

Hughes, Edward, 16

Hughs, Joseph, 17, 45

Hunt, Jonathan, 100

Hunter, James, 14, 16, 17

Huntsville, 92

Hus, John, 39

Husbands, Herman, 13, 16, 17, 37

Hutton, James, 38

J

Jack, Captain James, 33

Jackson, Dr., 113

Jefferson, Thomas, 108

K

Kapp, Jacob, 71

Kentucky, 82

Kinchen, Senator John: attacks Moravians, 69–70; changes mind about Moravians, 71

Kings Mountain, 86, 93, 95, 105; battle of, 88–89

Kiss of Peace, 73

Krause, Gottlob, 129

L

Labor strike: in Salem, 72, 73

Land Arbeiter Conferenz, 127

Land Confiscation Act of 1777, 62

Land controversies. See Moravians, land problems of

Lanier, Robert, 60

Lapp, Captain, 113

Lenoir, Captain William: antagonism toward Moravians, 104–15 passim; threatens Moravians, 104; as president of state senate, 104; as member of University of North Carolina board of trustees, 105; described, 105; menaces Traugott Bagge, 111–12; warned by Colonel William Campbell, 114

Lewis, Major Micajah, 111

Lexington, Massachusetts: battle of, 32

Liberty men. See Whigs

Lincoln County, 111

Lindsay's Plantation, 100

Loesch, Jacob, 15, 16

Lords Proprietors of Carolina, 6

Lot: explanation of, 23–24; declines in favor, 129

Loyalists. See Tories

M

McLeod, Captain Donald, 45

Manakes Hill, 123

Marshall, Frederic William, 4–5, 23; attends international church synod in Europe, 5; celebrates birthday of George III, 21–22; describes building of Salem, 27; comments on Bethabara Tory hunt, 84; as sympathetic with British, 103; entertains Cornwallis, 108; as leader of Moravians, 117; entertains state legislators, 121; describes plight of country in post-Revolutionary era, 125; death of, 131

at Cowan's Ford, 97; at Guilford Court-
house, 98, 100; criticized by General
Nathanael Greene, 98, 100. *See also*
Whigs, exactions from Moravians
North Carolina Provincial Congress, 30,
34–35, 51, 56; enacts test oath, 49
North Carolina Supreme Court, 63, 105

O

Oath of allegiance: described, 60–71 pas-
sim
Oath of abjurgation. *See* Oath of Al-
legiance
Old Richmond, 50
Old Town. *See* Bethabara
Orange County: political disorders in, 13
Outlyers, 45, 88

P

Pacifism, 5; Moravian views of, 35–37
Paper currency. *See* Moravians, currency
problems of
Partisan warfare, 51, 58–59, 83, 84, 87–88,
89–94; Bishop John Michael Graff's
reaction to, 58
Patriots. *See* Whigs
Peace of Paris, 5
Pearson, Richmond, 87
Peter, John Frederick, 112, 124
Petersburg, Virginia, 29
Pfeil, Jacob, 85
Pickens, General Andrew, 100
Pickens Militia: organized, 100; in Salem,
111, 114
Pilgrim Economy. *See* Moravians, com-
mon housekeeping of
Pindell, Richard, 113
Pitt, William the Elder, 116
Potter's shop: in Salem, 28, 29, 75
Praetzel, Gottfried, 71
Predestination, 11
Presbyterians, 10, 69
Preston, Colonel John, 113, 114
Psalm of Joy, 124

Q

Quakers, 10, 36, 37, 38, 40
Quartering: Parliament's role in, 115; in
Wachovia, 115–18
Queensware, 28
Quitrents, 6

R

Ramsour's Mill: battle of 83, 89
Read, Nathan, 84
Red Tannery, 29, 75
Regulators, 5; complaints of, 6–7; at odds

with Moravians, 7, 12, 15–16; excesses
of, 12, 13; and Hillsborough riot, 14, 19;
defeated at Alamance Creek, 16–17;
swear allegiance to Crown, 21, and be-
friended by Moravians, 21
Reuter, Christian: seeks site for Salem,
23–24; criticizes Traugott Bagge, 64
Reutz, Johannes, 114
Richmond: county seat of Surry County,
50, 53; raided by Tories, 89
Rowan County, 52, 80; division of, 50; as
Whig stronghold, 83; crossed by
British, 100
Rutherford, General Griffith: as leader of
expedition against Cherokees, 52, 105;
as chairman of joint House-Senate
committee, 68–69; as critic of Moravian
neutrality, 68; opposes Moravian petition, 69; as Rowan militia leader, 83

S

Saal: in Salem, 120
Salem, 40, 41, 43, 45, 47, 51, 80, 81, 101;
founding of, 23–31; and search for
building site, 23–24; as largest town
and leading commercial center of
Carolina backcountry, 26–27; described, 27, 107; rumors in, 43, 110; disturbances in, 52–53, 59, 83, 85–86,
104–15; Declaration of Independence
posted in, 55; drought in, 56; smallpox
epidemic in, 81–82; visited by Daniel
Boone, 82; liberty sentiment in, 103–4;
confiscations of British in, 110; receives
news of peace, 122; celebrates Easter
sunrise service, 122–23; celebrates
Fourth of July, 124–25; impact of freedom on, 127–34; breakdown of dress
codes in, 128–29
Salem *Diaconie*, 30, 75
Salem Tavern, 75; disturbances in, 52–53,
59; described, 58–59
Salisbury, 13, 17, 24, 27, 53, 80
Salisbury Committee of Safety, 48, 52, 54,
56
Sauratown Mountains, 87
Saxony, 20
Schaaf, Jeremias, 85
Schmidt, Captain Heinrich, 35, 51
Schneider, Martin, 85
Schober, Gottlieb: at odds with Traugott
Bagge, 65, 131; as apostle of American
"spirit of freedom," 129–31; as Mora-
vian spokesman in Wilkes County land
suit, 131; as justice of peace and state
senator, 131; appointed to *Aufseher
Collegium*, 131

menaces Moravians, 104–15 passim;
ordered out of Salem by Captain Joseph
Graham, 111–12; menaces Traugott
Bagge, 111–12
Williams, Colonel Joseph, 34, 51, 92–93
Wilmington, 20, 21, 43, 44, 45, 119
Winnsboro, South Carolina, 95
Winston, Major Joseph, 110–11; offers to
help Moravians, 113
Woodmason, Charles: quoted, 8, 9
Wright, Gideon, 87; background of, 50;
relationship to Martin Armstrong,
50–51; raises Tory army, 89–91; de-
feated at Shallow Ford, 92; death of, 93

Y
Yadkin County, 92
Yadkin River, 5, 8, 50, 91, 104; crossed by
American army, 98; crossed by British,
98, 100
Yarrell, Peter, 31, 75, 117
Yorktown, 100, 118

Z
Zeist, The Netherlands, 4
Zevely, Van Nemen, 129
Zillman, Heinrich, 117
Zinzendorf, Count Lewis, 3–4; leads fight
for Moravian exemptions, 39, 40
Zwingli, Ulrich, 11